FIRST BREATH OF MORNING

Where God Waits for You Every Day

A 90-Day Devotional

To Marge

Kathy Cheek

Psalm 63:1

Seek Him Early!

ENDORSEMENTS

FIRST BREATH OF MORNING

Where God Waits for You Every Day

A 90-Day Devotional

KATHY CHEEK

Cover and Interior Design: Derinda Babcock
Editor(s): Sue Fairchild, Deb Haggerty
Author Represented by Credo Communications

PUBLISHED BY: Elk Lake Publishing, Inc., 35 Dogwood Dr., Plymouth, MA 02360, 2018

Library Cataloging Data
Names: Cheek, Kathy (Kathy Cheek)
First Breath of Morning: Where God Waits for You Every Day/ Kathy Cheek
172 p. 23cm × 15cm (9in × 6 in.)
Description: *First Breath of Morning* is a multi-themed book of six chapters with multiple devotionals that portray a beautiful picture of our walk with God. Themes include drawing near, growing our relationship, leaning into His love, strengthening our faith, trusting Him through every circumstance, and exalting Him in worship. The messages in *First Breath of Morning* will refresh your faith and renew your trust in God.
Identifiers: ISBN-13: 978-1-948888-52-3 (trade) | 978-1-948888-51-6 (POD) | 978-1-948888-53-0 (e-book.)
Key Words: Prayer, Faith, Fellowship, Grace, Love, Worship, Adoration
LCCN: 2018954835 Nonfiction

DEDICATION

When I was first trying to become a published writer, I was writing children's material including stories, poetry, plays and skits. For a long time, I submitted these pieces to magazines and church curriculum publishers. *Everything was passed up and rejected.*

In a moment of deep discouragement, I threw away everything I'd written. I opened manila folders containing the stories and poems, plays and skits and tore them into tiny little pieces and took them out in the trash. They were gone. This was right before my husband purchased our first computer, so there was no back up resource that contained any copies of anything I'd written.

It didn't take very long for regret to set in. I was ashamed of myself for throwing my writing away. Months went by and I didn't write anything. *It felt like that dream was completely gone.*

More time passed, and I realized I missed writing but I still experienced the regret and shame. I prayed a prayer I will never forget. I shared my heart with the Lord and *asked Him to forgive me* for throwing away everything I'd written. *I humbly asked Him to please restore my writing and I knew it was in His hands to answer as He chose.*

Shortly after that while sitting at my new computer, I let my thoughts go blank with fingers on the keyboard, and suddenly, I was typing words I hadn't planned. I typed one sentence which turned into a page filled with lines of words I don't remember putting much thought into and before I knew it a poem stared back at me from the monitor. *It was an inspirational poem about waiting on the Lord.*

Until that day, I had not written any inspirational poetry. But since that day, I have been writing inspirational poetry, devotions, and articles, and after a long journey that involved many rejections along the way, I began to be published in several Christian magazines, and now, my first book is out.

God answered my prayer and restored my writing! From a heart of gratitude, I dedicate *First Breath of Morning* to the Lord and pray His power and blessing falls on every word.

ACKNOWLEDGMENTS

I wish I could thank my English teacher in high school, who saw something in my writing in the mid-1970s, but I didn't believe in myself enough to see what she saw or to understand the gifts God gives us to use for His purpose. Her words echoed in the far recesses of my mind like a swift flicker of light through the passage of the years reminding me there was a writer inside me. I would say to myself, someday, maybe someday.

I will thank the ones who brought my vision to life in *First Breath of Morning*. At the top of the list is Deb Haggerty of Elk Lake Publishing Inc. Thank you, Deb, for embracing this devotional because you saw something unique in the book. Thanks to Karen Neumair, my agent at Credo Communications, for helping forge the path to bring everything together and for offering support in many areas, a number of which I am still learning. An important thank you goes to Sue Fairchild, who used her editor's skill like a potter with clay. She "molded and trimmed" this manuscript until the finished product that was meant to be emerged from her potter's wheel.

Of course, I want to say thank you to my family. My husband, Randy, who has always supported my writing and strongly believes in this book, and to my daughters, Amy and Mary, who have continually encouraged me to follow my writing dreams wherever they lead.

A NOTE FROM THE AUTHOR

A rewarding journey to discover what the Lord has for us through his love, through faith, and relationship with him.

My pursuit of a deeper understanding of God's love, faith, and walking with him, took place as I journeyed to find my way through a time of feeling confused and without direction. Many of us have been at a crossroads in our faith walk where we choose to go deeper in our relationship with God and wholly follow after him or continue our own path in our own way.

First Breath of Morning is what I wrote in that journey as I sought the Lord through a more intensive time alone with him and in his Word and discovered that finding him was much more rewarding than finding myself. And in drawing closer to him, he revealed who he made me to be.

I made a stronger commitment to my regular quiet time and in that time with God, I learned the importance of developing a deeper relationship with him, and I discovered the depth of his love and found the stronger faith he calls us to when we yield surrendered lives unto him. He taught me he is there for us in all our struggles and conflicts and we are never alone, he is always with us. This is a journey God wants us all to take and it is a journey of love, faith, trust, surrender, obedience, and wholly following our Lord.

My greatest desire is for God's love to pour off these pages and into your heart, for I believe it is in knowing he has a deep abiding love for us that motivates us to walk in close relationship with him. This is when we will experience his presence working in our lives, and we will find our faith and trust growing deeper day by day.

In Christ's Deep Abiding Love,
Kathy Cheek

CONTENTS

CHAPTER ONE

MORNING INVITATION

Morning is an invitation from the Lord to start the day with him,
Then spend the day inviting him to walk with you each
step of the way.

A day I start with you, Lord,

Is a day I stay with you.

First Breath of Morning

Have you not known?
Have you not heard?
The everlasting God, the LORD,
The Creator of the ends of the earth,
Neither faints nor is weary.
His understanding is unsearchable.

—Isaiah 40:28

He who never wearies,
Never slumbers, never sleeps,
Leans over heaven
First breath of morning
And wakens me with his amazing love.

Nothing inspires me more than this: knowing the Lord is waiting for us each day; knowing that every morning he invites us to meet with him, talk with him, and go through our day with him. For me, my day always begins with the first breath of morning. In the quiet, waking moments of each new morning, before the rest of the world comes rushing in, I hear his voice and I know he is near. *The first breath of each new morning is where he waits for me—and for you.*

He will not allow your foot to be moved:
He who keeps you will not slumber.
Behold, He who keeps Israel
Shall neither slumber nor sleep.

—Psalm 121:3-4

The Beauty of Morning

My soul waits for the Lord
More than those who watch for the morning—
Yes, more than those who watch for the morning.

—Psalm 130:6

I caught the sky in a moment of beauty this morning. As I opened the blinds on the east side of the house, the beautiful skies drew me outside to catch a better view. Yesterday's morning sky was hazy, but today's was a lovely palette for my morning heart.

I love to watch the sunlight spread across the sky, ushering in the newness that lies ahead for yet another day. Morning surrounds me and ushers in a fresh intimacy with the Lord as I stand under the vast expanse of his creation with nothing at all between us. I know his Spirit lives inside of me, and when I am standing beneath a big, beautiful morning sky, I also know he is all around me. That is what I take with me through the rest of the day.

The beauty of morning was birthed in my heart several years ago when I began, day by day and dawn by dawn, running to meet my Lord, and embracing the blessings his presence poured into my life. Each day, he filled me to overflowing while simultaneously filling me with a thirst for more.

As we choose to place our first thoughts upon him each morning, we begin the day with the joy that can only come from walking in close relationship to the Lord. The beauty of morning is the treasure of more of him.

Morning is a wonderful time to find great joy in who God is and to discover anew the overflowing abundance of his love, grace, and mercy.

A Quiet Lesson

Be still, and know that I am God;
I will be exalted among the nations,
I will be exalted in the earth!

—Psalm 46:10

I was single and in my early twenties, sitting in church on a Sunday morning—a Sunday morning I will always remember. I feel certain the pastor who included this Scripture about being still and knowing God in his message would never know the deep impact this message would have on my life. For me, the Scripture was to be the beginning of a deeper relationship with the Lord—one I didn't even know was possible. The pastor quoted the widely known "be still" verse, and then said, "We have so much noise in our lives—how can we even hear God when he desires to speak to us?"

His message instantly convicted me. I knew God wanted me to pay close attention to the lesson he had for me in the pastor's message. What penetrated the deepest in my heart was my need for more time to be still in order to talk to God, and also time to listen for his voice. I had been resisting quiet in my lifestyle. I always had music on or a television making noise in my apartment. As soon as I slid into my car, I would quickly turn on the radio.

But after that message, I changed my habits. When I slid into my car, I didn't immediately turn on the radio. When I arrived home to my quiet apartment, I didn't turn on anything right away except the lights. In the morning, when I was putting on my makeup and styling my hair, I didn't have the television or radio on in the background. These changes added more silence into my routine, and I discovered I began to spend more time in prayer and engaged in meaningful conversation with the Lord.

As a result of spending quiet time communing with God, I drew nearer to him. This closeness gave me a sense of belonging to him I had not experienced before and caused me to want to spend more time with him. I had greater peace and joy in my life because I had gained a deeper insight into who I was as a child of God. He opened my eyes to many new lessons

I was eager to learn, and thus began a journey that took me through years of walking in close relationship with my heavenly Father.

How can you know him, child of God, unless you spend time with him? How can you know—really know—who you are if you aren't in close communion with the one who made you, loves you, and has a plan for your life?

> When You said, "Seek My face,"
> My heart said to You, "Your face, LORD, I will seek."
>
> —Psalm 27:8

More

Now it happened as they went that He entered a certain village; and a certain woman named Martha welcomed Him into her house. And she had a sister called Mary, who also sat at Jesus' feet and heard His word. But Martha was distracted with much serving, and she approached Him and said, "Lord, do You not care that my sister has left me to serve alone? Therefore tell her to help me." And Jesus answered and said to her, "Martha, Martha, you are worried and troubled about many things. But one thing is needed, and Mary has chosen that good part, which will not be taken away from her."

—Luke 10:38-42

Our days are often filled with busyness, distractions, obligations, and activities too many to number, until our hours and moments quickly pass by, and an entire day comes to an end before we realize we haven't spent time alone with the Lord. Our plan wasn't to let time slip away like that, but it did anyway. In all the blur of too much busyness, what are we missing when we don't intentionally and diligently make the time to pull ourselves away from everything else to spend quality time with him?

One-on-one personal time with the Lord is a gift that affords us the opportunity to know him. Time with him is the path to a relationship that can be compared to no other on this earth, because it isn't of this earth—it is supernatural and divine. God uniquely created and designed us to have a rich and intimate relationship with him. But we have to make that relationship a priority in our busy lives.

My desire to spend time with him is evidence I am his child and we are connected. His Spirit lives in me. The more time I spend with my heavenly Father, the more I understand the amazing implications of this truth.

More than prayer and more than studying his Word, just setting aside time to be still in his presence yields a close relationship with God. All are important, but one is—more. Sit at his feet every day, pour out your heart to him, listen as he pours back into you, and you will know him—*more*.

New Day, New Slate

Through the Lord's mercies we are not consumed,
Because His compassions fail not.
They are new every morning;
Great is Your faithfulness.

—Lamentations 3:22-23

Yes, we are immeasurably blessed!
God's mercy is new every morning,
And you will know it when you meet with Him
Each new day.

You will know the slate is clean, with no traces remaining of yesterday. A fresh, clean slate holds the promise of a better day to come. The beginning of a brand new day offers a fresh start. You will know there are new beginnings with new opportunities and new horizons.

His love is also new every morning. Mercy is often translated in the Bible as lovingkindness, and isn't that the best kind of love? We have a God whose love is patient and kind, and his mercy is new and easy to be found when you meet with him every morning of each new day. His love is merciful, and his mercy demonstrates his unending love to us.

There have been times when I've had a miserable day and couldn't wait to simply go to bed, knowing when I woke up the next morning, a new day awaited me—a new day to do things better. The truth is, God's mercy is available every moment. If I mess up in the morning or in the afternoon, I can start anew in that very moment I say, "Lord, I'm sorry. I need to hit the refresh button on this day and start again in a place of new mercy."

Morning Invitation

Cause me to hear Your lovingkindness in the morning,
For in You do I trust;
Cause me to know the way in which I should walk,
For I lift up my soul to You.

—Psalm 143:8

As I wake and lazily toss my head on my soft, comfy pillow when another early morning beckons me, I know it's time to wake up, leave the warm and cozy covers, and get on with my day.

But there is something more beckoning me—an invitation, a voice so familiar, a gentle voice I've heard before, that clears away the foggy sleep and says, "I am here. Wake up to me."

Ah, yes, I remember … waking up each morning is more than just diving into another day and a long to-do list. Waking up is about another day of journey with the Lord, another day of rejoicing in my Father's presence, another day of taking his hand and walking with him by my side—guiding, leading, and loving me.

No other invitation or opportunity could possibly come close to the one that is lovingly sent to me each morning!

And so, upon waking, before my eyes even open or my feet slip to the floor, before I make a cup of coffee, before I start my day, I will accept his morning invitation and choose to start my day with him. I breathe in this brand-new day with a smile on my waking face and in my waking heart.

I love the fresh start of morning.
In newness the day ushers in
Loving kindness from your hand,
And a balm for my soul.
I'll leave yesterday behind,
And start anew this day with you.

BEFORE I PRAY

Likewise the Spirit also helps in our weaknesses. For we do not know what we should pray for as we ought, but the Spirit Himself makes intercession for us with groanings which cannot be uttered. Now He who searches the hearts knows what the mind of the Spirit is, because He makes intercession for the saints according to the will of God.

—Romans 8:26-27

By the time I arrive at my "official prayer time," I have already been *praying* many things. I have already engaged in much conversation with the Lord, who hears my prayers before I utter them and knows my thoughts and words before I express them.

Before I sit in my favorite seat by the window for this special time with the Lord, I have already welcomed a new morning and thanked him for this new day. Before I even meet him in our designated place, I have already placed my day in his hands and asked his blessing on all I do.

We've already started our day together, and his rhythm of grace is already beating strong in me. I heard his whisper as soon as waking moments brought me out of the night's slumber and I eagerly welcomed the break of yet another dawn.

Through the motions and routines of the beginning of a new day, I have already invited him fully into mine and drawn near to him. But a special time and place still wait for me, set aside to lay all my cares into his hands. That's when I call upon him to intercede on the behalf of loved ones and anyone I know who has a specific need. This designated, intentional time with the Lord has long been a habit of mine. My day wouldn't be right or complete without it. I cannot deprive my day of this.

Even before we "pray," we can be in conversation with the Lord. First Thessalonians 5:17 exhorts us to "pray without ceasing." Prayer—like words—can fall like breath from our lips and from our hearts. Prayer is the language God most readily hears.

GETTING TO KNOW HIM

As the deer pants for the water brooks,
So pants my soul for You, O God.

—Psalm 42:1

Why, upon rising early in the morning, do I begin a conversation with the Lord that will continue throughout the day? Because, knowing him better than ever before, I can't imagine going through my day any other way. I know my heavenly Father better than I did before because I spend time with him every day.

I haven't always been this way. I have not always pursued the close relationship with the Lord I knew he desired to have with me. But he kept pulling at my heart and calling my name, and his love and grace built a foundation for a deeper walk with him.

Getting closer isn't complicated. A deep relationship with the one who loves you most consists of talking to him, quietly listening to him, praying, reading his Word, meditating on all he speaks to your heart, and praising him for all he means to you—and, if you're like me, all he means is a very long list!

Some days I don't ask for anything.
Some days I don't bring any petition before him.
Some days I just praise him.
Some days I just sit quietly before him.

Just me and my Lord. My privilege and joy is to open to him my grateful heart and express all the praise and thanksgiving that lives and breathes inside of me. The more time I spend with him, the better I know him. The better I know him, the more I love him and want to spend time with him. That's why I eagerly begin an engaging conversation with him upon waking each morning—a conversation that continues throughout my day. And morning is just the beginning ... oh, but what a beginning!

SANCTUARY

For thus says the LORD GOD, the Holy One of Israel:
"In returning and rest you shall be saved;
In quietness and confidence shall be your strength."
—Isaiah 30:15

For me, quiet thoughts are a sweet savor. Yet, to have quiet thoughts, there must first be quiet moments. Quiet thoughts and quiet moments are my sanctuary.

And one of my favorite sanctuaries, besides my official prayer spot, where quiet thoughts and quiet moments reign, is the beautiful trail near my home where I can walk in woods and along the creek. There, I breathe differently, I think differently, and I pray differently. I talk to my heavenly Father as he comes along beside me with every step I take. This is special to me.

Most of the people I pass are plugged in and listening to something or are on their phones, and I sometimes wonder if they ever experience quiet moments or quiet thoughts. I, too, would miss the beauty of quiet moments if I let myself be swept along in life's swift current and didn't make the time.

But I have heard his voice calling me to this.

Sometimes, those moments come as I sit by a window, gazing at a sky that promises his return someday. Other times, they come as I linger in my small backyard garden that is a sanctuary to birds, rabbits, and squirrels … and to my quiet, breathing heart.

Sometimes they come as I'm gazing out the car window on a long and open road.

Sometimes they come in footsteps that carry me down a winding path.

But I have heard his voice calling me to this. He is teaching this heart of mine to be still.

The Most Important Thing

Glory in His holy name;
Let the hearts of those rejoice who seek the LORD!
Seek the LORD and His strength;
Seek His face evermore!

—Psalm 105:3-4

Nothing clears my head more than this—a walk in wide, open spaces with fresh air filling my lungs while I'm having a conversation with God. In this place where there is nothing between us, I can fully embrace being present with the Lord. I wouldn't trade this for anything in the world.

Sometimes I forget how carefully I must guard what is so precious to me—taking time to steal away quietly and deeply focus, putting away thoughts of everything else and drawing near to the Lord.

Getting caught up in activities, even good ones, can take us down a road where we find ourselves involved in too many things, all going on at the same time. And, before we know, time has slipped away, and we have not made time for the most important thing. Consistently making time to be alone with God is an essential quest that requires a setting of boundaries on the time we give to the different pursuits of our lives.

Stealing a moment with God is not that hard, really. The time may be sipping coffee on your back porch and watching a sunrise or sunset, enjoying the wonder to the fullest because you are sharing the view with the one who made those beautiful skies.

That moment might be a song that stirs your thoughts, drawing you near to God.

We all have them—divine encounters that mean something special to us. As our days unfold before us, let us choose to guard those intimate moments when we most enjoy our relationship with God.

We need to
Make Time
and
Take Time
to
Spend Time
with God alone.

This is the most important thing we can do.

A Thousand to One

Be still, and know that I am God;
I will be exalted among the nations,
I will be exalted in the earth!

—Psalm 46:10

It's quiet here this morning;
Yet a thousand thoughts
Are tumbling in my mind.
As I draw near to him,
He brings my thousand thoughts
Down to one …
Be still, and know that I am God!

Every time I read Psalm 46:10, my heart hears this message: Be still and know me … *really* know me.

I believe this goes a step beyond knowing he is God—it's a step toward knowing him as *God of your life* and getting to know him in close relationship. The closeness starts with knowing and acknowledging that he is God. Then really knowing him grows into knowing him in the intimate relationship of Father and child.

This has been a life-changing message for me, as I've learned to be still and spend time with my God. My heart greatly desires to obey this message, because I know the benefits that come with this intimate knowledge. My prayer is I will consistently and diligently choose to be still and know him throughout my entire life.

Being still brings me into his presence and causes me to know his nearness. As you continue to draw near to God, who has shown you grace and mercy through his love, you will also discover the relationship you share takes on new meaning.

Don't let all the duties, activities, and distractions in life rob you of this precious relationship. Knowing him is life. Make time for him. *Let him bring your thousand thoughts down to one.* Be still and know him. Be still and know he is your God.

Near

The LORD is near to all who call upon Him,
To all who call upon Him in truth.

—Psalm 145:18

I want to be counted among those who intentionally draw near to Jesus—near to the one who saved us, loves us, and pours immeasurable grace and mercy into our lives—the one who leads and guides us, strengthens us, and never leaves us alone.

I remember others long before me who are known for drawing near.

I remember Mary, at the feet of Jesus.

I remember John, the beloved disciple, leaning on the chest of our Lord.

I remember David, the psalmist whose soul thirsted for God.

I remember Enoch, walking close beside him—so close, in fact, that God just walked him on up to heaven, completely bypassing death.

The list could go on and on. I want my name to be included with those who have deeply desired intimate communion and fellowship with the Lord. Don't you?

I want to draw near to the Lord who wakens me each morning and reminds me that this new day he has made is a day to be glad. *And I am glad*—deep-in-my-heart glad that I am his and he is mine. I am grateful that I have the privilege of walking in close relationship with him.

Let's live each day *for him* and *with him* and be counted *near. There is no better place to be.*

SAVOR

In quietness and confidence shall be your strength.
—Isaiah 30:15b

Have you ever just sat silent and still for a little while, with quietness wrapped around you like a comforting favorite blanket? If you have, you know the stillness can become a moment that invokes an atmosphere of peace.

How did that happen? Well, the world slowed down because you slowed down. Calm had a chance to breathe.

When I sit still and silent, I close my eyes and breathe deeply this gift of serenity, for just a little while.

Sometimes we all need a little time to truly catch our breath …

Just for a little while, we need quiet, peaceful moments to hear ourselves think the deep thoughts—thoughts that compete for our attention but stay hidden in the shadows, because they have been crowded out by our busyness.

But for a little while *savor your deep thoughts* and listen to what your heart wants you to hear.

You know the thoughts I'm talking about. Maybe a prayer for someone. Maybe an idea, a dream, a hope you have felt stirring. Maybe letting go of piled-up stress that needs to be exhaled and released. Maybe acknowledging God's nearness and drawing close to him.

Don't pick that phone up again. The call can wait. This is a moment for stillness. The innermost part of your heart is trying to tell you something. You need this. From time to time, we all need this.

We need to give ourselves permission to savor quiet, restful moments.

They will refresh you. They will remind you who you are. You will have a new outlook on life and all that is going on around you.

All you have to do is be still … for a little while.

What If

My voice You shall hear in the morning, O LORD;
In the morning I will direct it to You,
And I will look up.

—Psalm 5:3

When you woke up this morning, what was your first thought? What was your first awareness as the fog of sleep began to lift?

Did you have a troubled and worrisome thought, the one you fell asleep with, the one that caused you to toss and turn throughout the night? Was the thought a to-do list you wish was already done? Were you feeling guilty over what you didn't finish yesterday?

Were you thinking about the dozens of emails in your inbox, many still unread and far too many still unanswered?

Did a hundred thoughts scramble for your attention before your feet even touched the floor?

What if you pushed all of those aside, as hard as that can be?

What if, before all of those thoughts took over your morning, you turned your thoughts to the Lord?

What if the first words you uttered were, "Good morning, Lord."?

What if you stopped and thought first about his presence, ever near you?

What if you remembered you were not alone? Would you thank him for this day and tell him you're grateful he is near?

When your feet hit the floor after you already had this early morning conversation with him, would you feel his strength surging deep inside your heart? You would, because that is who he is.

He is the Lord who waits to be invited into your day. And as soon as you awaken, he is there waiting for you, holding out his beckoning hand.

What if, when you wake up each morning, you reach out your hand to his and call upon his name?

THE QUIET PLACE

There is a place
Where I can go,
A quiet place
Where I can know
The awe and wonder of Almighty God.

And in this place
He meets with me,
And in this place
He lets me see
The glory and the beauty of his love.

I love this place,
This quiet place,
It's where I want to be.

The world is busy rushing by,
So much to do,
So much to gain,
So many places to be.

Not for me.
I'd rather be …

There is a place
Where I can go,
A quiet place
Where I can know …

All his mercy,
All his love,

All his mercy,
All his love.

CHAPTER TWO

The Seeker

My heart holds a treasure
The whole world seeks,
I found it in seeking you.

A Walk of the Heart

And you will seek Me and find Me, when you search for Me with all your heart.

—Jeremiah 29:13

My soul ever longs to closer be,
My heart seeks to know you more.

One morning, I declared in my journal that each day was a brand-new day to walk with the Lord. Then, as I paused to consider and examine what those words truly meant, I realized much of that "walking" is through my thoughts and prayers as I seek him each day. This "walking" can be accomplished without taking one single step. Walking with the Lord is a walk that takes place in the heart—a heart that follows him.

I went on to write in my journal, "Today, walking with him required that I not worry about something troubling that happened, but to pray and trust. Today, walking with him has shown me through the reading of his Word that I am not helpless, but I am an overcomer and more than a conqueror."

Walking with the Lord has also taught me to never give up when visible answers to prayer are slow in coming. Walking with him has shown me this week not to focus on the natural things of this world or the circumstances surrounding me, but to keep my eyes on God and what only he can do.

Our journey with the Lord is a daily walk of seeking him in prayer and trusting him in all things. This is a walk of the heart we must choose to take each brand-new day.

ABBA FATHER

For you did not receive the spirit of bondage again to fear, but you received the Spirit of adoption by whom we cry out, "Abba, Father." The Spirit Himself bears witness with our spirit that we are children of God, and if children, then heirs—heirs of God and joint heirs with Christ, if indeed we suffer with Him, that we may also be glorified together.

—Romans 8:15-17

Abba
I have sought him, and he drew near;
He drew me into loving arms.
Finally, I am home.

What mere words could possibly describe the glorious relationship we can enter into with our Abba Father? He eagerly awaits a heart that desires to draw close to him. He cherishes each and every moment we choose to spend with him.

He delights in our presence, just as we delight in his. His Father's heart is always open to us when we talk to him, laugh, cry, and talk some more. He listens and gives us himself in return.

In my experience with people, establishing relationships aren't that easy. Sometimes they are hard work,
And sometimes they don't work at all.

With our Abba Father, we don't have to work—we just seek him. Seek him with all your heart, and you will find him. Know him, and you will find everlasting love. Enjoy his fellowship, and you will find intimacy. Build a relationship with him, and you will find a loving Father.

Glory in His holy name;
Let the hearts of those rejoice who seek the LORD!
Seek the LORD and His strength;
Seek His face evermore!

—Psalm 105:3-4

Behold what manner of love the Father has bestowed on us,
that we should be called children of God!

—1 John 3:1

Two Places

But seek first the kingdom of God and His righteousness,
and all these things shall be added to you.
—Matthew 6:33

I recently examined what guides me as I navigate life and asked myself these two questions: *What goes on within me? What goes on around me?*

I decided to break them down and take a closer look.

What goes on within me?

Faith.

God.

What goes on around me?

The world.

Circumstances.

I asked myself again: *What truly guides me in this world I live in?* I decided there are two places I can stand as I navigate through the world—I can stand by faith in a faithful God or I can stand in the world and be stuck in circumstances controlled by the world. Circumstances can have tremendous sway on us if we aren't standing firmly with God.

The first place is where my heart lives. Faith resides there—a place where I faithfully trust in God and trust that every single detail will come together as he has planned. Because of who he is and my relationship with him, I have trusted that he will work *all* out for my good and his glory, knowing I have sought his wisdom and guidance and that my circumstances have been covered with prayer.

The second place is this world we live in, and it's a world filled with circumstances that constantly swirl around us. There are often pressures and struggles associated with the things of this world. Some are normal, everyday events, and others are unexpected challenges. We must navigate our way through everything, even though we are often uncertain about what to do and which choice to make.

We have a choice—will we stand firmly in the first place or go to the second? When we stand in the place of faith, God works to accomplish his will. He is in control. Prayer is answered. He is far superior to the circumstances of this life in which we are woefully entangled. Sometimes he untangles things, straightens them out, and shows us his power and strength. Other times, he carries us through the tangled web and changes us in the process to be more like him. Either way, we are immensely blessed, and he will be glorified.

Seek him first—this is how we stand firmly in the first place.

Additional verses:

Psalm16:11, Psalm 25:4-5, Psalm 37:23, Proverbs 3:5-6, James 1:5, 1 John 5:4

A Masterpiece in the Mirror

For we are His workmanship, created in Christ Jesus for good works, which God prepared beforehand that we should walk in them.

—Ephesians 2:10

The twelve of us were a mixed group of all ages as we met for a study of Ephesians on Tuesday nights, but we were all also serious seekers of truth in God's Word. As a result, we had exceptionally engaging discussions around the questions at the end of each chapter. One question in the study guide at the end of chapter two asked, "If you told someone at work or school that you are a masterpiece, or a work of art, what would they probably say?"

We knew that one young lady in our group didn't esteem herself very highly, and sure enough she said, "No one would think I was a masterpiece! They would just laugh at me and say, 'That's stupid!'" We could hear the pain in her answer but appreciated her open and honest reply. We delved into quite an illuminating discussion, hoping she would receive the truth of this verse in Scripture.

After our discussion, the young lady transformed right in front of our eyes. Her entire countenance changed. She smiled, and her face lit up, because she saw herself as God sees her—possibly for the first time in her life. She now understood this verse was her assurance she was created and designed by God and he has great plans for her life.

During the next week, she continued to absorb the truth she had learned and the realization that she was, indeed, God's workmanship, created for good works. She walked into our class the next week a different person. She stood taller, seemed more confident and self-assured. She smiled more, and even her tone was different. What a difference a week made! There was now a new glow beaming from a face that had been downcast just the week before.

This young lady's encounter with the biblical truth about her beauty and value to God had turned a light on inside her that life's circumstances had dimmed. Her negative view of herself was transformed as she began looking at herself through the eyes of Scripture. She told us she even smiled when she looked at herself in the mirror now, and she quoted Ephesians 2:10, which had become her favorite verse.

OUTWARD APPEARANCE

> But the LORD said to Samuel, "Do not look at his appearance or at his physical stature, because I have refused him. For the LORD does not see as man sees; for man looks at the outward appearance, but the LORD looks at the heart."
>
> —1 Samuel 16:7

When the prophet Samuel was sent to anoint a king to replace Saul, and Jesse paraded his sons before him, God refused the one Samuel thought he would choose. In so doing, God made a very powerful statement about looking at outward appearance versus looking at what is in a person's heart. Samuel had taken one look at Eliab and said, "Surely the Lord's anointed is before Him." God quickly corrected his error in assumption. A few verses later, God makes clear he had chosen David, and David—not Eliab—was the one anointed to be the next king of Israel.

In the very next chapter, we get a close-up look at David's heart as he went out to fight Goliath when, without hesitation, he declares, "The battle is the Lord's!" We see his strong faith and confidence in the Lord, and we see his deep courage in living out that faith as he took on the giant with a mere slingshot and five simple stones.

When I read in the Bible that God is more interested in our inner beauty than our outer beauty, I am rejuvenated and encouraged. If my value were determined only on my outward appearance, I'm afraid our world wouldn't attribute great worth to my life.

Outward appearance refers to more than just our physical attributes. I would include the things we do to appear outwardly that we are of great value. We often place too much significance on the material possessions we accumulate and the credentials and status we acquire.

Wouldn't you rather be rich in faith than rich in the things of this world? Wouldn't you prefer to acquire the riches found in sitting at the Lord's feet rather than the riches that accumulate in a big bank account? When God looks at your heart, don't you want him to see what he saw in David—a steadfast devotion and confidence in him? The courage to fight the battles of life, knowing the battle belongs to the Lord?

Then David said to the Philistine, "You come to me with a sword, with a spear, and with a javelin. But I come to you in the name of the LORD of hosts, the God of the armies of Israel, whom you have defied. This day the LORD will deliver you into my hand, and I will strike you and take your head from you. And this day I will give the carcasses of the camp of the Philistines to the birds of the air and the wild beasts of the earth, that all the earth may know that there is a God in Israel. Then all this assembly shall know that the LORD does not save with sword and spear; for the battle is the LORD's, and He will give you into our hands."

—1 Samuel 17:45-47

THIRST AND LIVING WATER

Jesus answered and said to her, "Whoever drinks of this water will thirst again, but whoever drinks of the water that I shall give him will never thirst. But the water that I shall give him will become in him a fountain of water springing up into everlasting life."

—John 4:13-14

There is a paved walking trail a few blocks from our house that winds like a ribbon next to a creek and the woods along its banks. A large bridge gives passage across the creek and offers a view of the gurgling, rippling waters flowing beneath. Shadowy trees rise above the steep, rock-lined banks of the stream.

During the drought of 2011, I kept checking on the creek. I dreaded the day I would peer over the side of the bridge and find the flow of water had stopped. Amazingly, despite the persistent lack of rain, the stream kept flowing all year. The water did drop to an extremely low level, but the pleasant singing of water passing under the bridge continued.

The creek reminded me of our Living Water—Jesus, the Water that never runs low. I thought about the thirst in our lives only he can quench. I thought about the satisfaction only he can bring. He is the answer to any drought in our lives; he holds the answer to all our needs. But first we must drink.

In every frustration, he comes to us with peace. He loves us and doesn't want us to stay in an agitated and bothered state. When we place the frustration in his hands, our thirst is quenched with calmness and peace.

When we are worried, he comes to us with rest and turns our fretting into trusting. When we are lonely, he promises to never leave us. When we are uncertain, he comes to us with truth and wisdom and opens our eyes to see more clearly.

When we don't know where to go, he invites us to follow him and trust wherever the path may lead.

When we drink of the Living Water that is Jesus, he pours all he is into us, and we are filled with him. Jesus is the Spring of Living Water and the River of Life that flows through us.

THE TROUBLE WITH CIRCUMSTANCES

And we know that all things work together for good to those who
love God, to those who are the called according to His purpose.
—Romans 8:28

Today, I fought discouragement,
Because I looked at me instead of God;
I looked at circumstances,
Instead of him.

But then, I fixed my gaze on him,
And by the time evening fell,
Discouragement had also fallen away.

Looking at our difficult circumstances can often get us into trouble.
When we examine what is going on around us, it's easy to think, *this is bad,
this is messed up, and there is no way it can be resolved.* We easily fall into the
trap of telling ourselves, *I don't see how God can work through this or fix it.*
Or we jump right into questioning why he let this happen in the first place.
When discouragement sets in, what are we to do?

The best attitude we can have is to be grateful. God can work in any
situation! Nothing is too big or too hard for him, and we don't have to face
any difficult situation alone.

How often we look at our circumstances in the natural, rather than
in the divine or supernatural, where God can work in powerful ways we
cannot even imagine. If we only have our own strength to rely on, then we
surely grow discouraged. But when we look to God, our hearts are filled
with hope and awe because we know he does great and mighty things.

The story of Joseph is one of the greatest examples in the Bible where
more is going on than what is seen in the circumstances. Joseph's brothers

plotted to murder him. But instead of killing him, they put him in a pit, then decide to sell him to slave traders. You know the rest of the story—he ends up falsely imprisoned for many years. Now that is a long string of difficult circumstances! Yet, if you read the whole story from Genesis 37 to 50, you will repeatedly see God's good hand of favor on Joseph through it all.

God delivered Joseph from prison and promoted him to the second in power in the land of Egypt. At God's prompting, Joseph wisely stored food and prepared for the coming famine. He was eventually reunited with his family, and there we see the most beautiful aspect of this whole story: Joseph forgave his brothers. The most memorable and oft repeated verse from this entire passage is Joseph's statement to his brothers in Genesis 50:20: *But as for you, you meant evil against me; but God meant it for good, in order to bring it about as it is this day, to save many people alive.*

Joseph's story, as do many other stories in the Bible, demonstrates to us how God is always working in those things we cannot see. God is continually working in and through bad circumstances for good.

Take your eyes off the circumstance and look at God.
The circumstance can overwhelm
Until you remind yourself again
Who God is and
Who you are in him.

By the Rivers of Water

A place of blessing
For those who delight in the Lord.

Blessed is the man
Who walks not in the counsel of the ungodly,
Nor stands in the path of sinners,
Nor sits in the seat of the scornful;
But his delight is in the law of the LORD,
And in His law he meditates day and night.
He shall be like a tree
Planted by the rivers of water,
That brings forth its fruit in its season,
Whose leaf also shall not wither;
And whatever he does shall prosper.

—Psalm 1:1-3

This passage begins our journey through the Psalms, a book largely written by David, which is filled with turmoil and triumph, tears and joy, battles and victories. What a great declaration we read in the first few verses of this chapter, reminding us of the blessing we have in our position of delighting in the Lord.

By the rivers of water,
This is where I want to be.

Wouldn't you love to be like the tree in verse three that is firmly planted by the rivers of water and is fruitful and prospers? Isn't this the life we want to live in the Lord? This is the life he has promised to those who walk in close relationship with him. This life starts with a choice: Will we choose to follow the ways of an ungodly world, or will we choose to delight in the Lord?

What does "delighting in the Lord" mean? Certainly more than having a casual relationship with him. Delight happens as a result of consistently spending time building a rich and fulfilling relationship with God that leaves you wanting more. Spending intimate time with the Lord enables you to grow in a faith that is steadfast and firm. If you seek the Lord and follow after him, you will delight in him. To know him is to delight in him.

What is your desire? Do you long to be firmly planted by the rivers of water, solid and secure, delighting in the Lord day by day?

THE LORD REIGNS

The Lord reigns, He is clothed with majesty;
The Lord is clothed,
He has girded Himself with strength.
Surely the world is established, so that it cannot be moved.
Your throne is established from of old;
You are from everlasting.

—Psalm 93:1-2

We often live, sometimes unintentionally, and sometimes very intentionally, as if we are in control of our own lives.

We are not in control. We are not lord over our own lives. Every ounce of our being cries out to be in charge of our lives, to fix everything. And yet that is the exact opposite of faith and trust. Control is completely contradictory with yielding and following. Control is totally contrary to making God the foundation of our lives.

When we build our lives on the foundation that is God and keep him at the center, he becomes our *whole* life—not just a part. He is our all in all.

When we continually grow in our walk with the Lord, we eventually find praying about everything first natural—not waiting until after we have exhausted all of our other resources. If we are doing everything in our own effort first, then we are still placing ourselves in the position of being lord of our own lives.

Do you ever pray in such a way that it sounds like you're telling God how he should fix things for you? I find myself falling into this pattern way too often, and I have to stop and surrender my will to his, acknowledging his sovereignty in my life and over my circumstances.

Another temptation is to view God's position as lord of our lives as a weakness. If we listen to what the world says, we may see our dependence on God as *giving up much* of ourselves, when the opposite is actually true. We will *gain much* when we put God first, because we release his power to work and flow more freely when we give him access to every corner of our hearts. *What others may perceive as a weakness is actually wisdom and strength on our part.*

Only when we give God full authority and allow him the rightful position of reigning as Lord over our lives do we see the person he uniquely designed emerge as he created us to be.

I Am Clay

But now, O LORD,
You are our Father;
We are the clay, and You our potter;
And all we are the work of Your hand.

—Isaiah 64:8

When you think of your favorite song or a favorite painting, you think of the finished product. The composer or artist has already conceived the idea, fashioned the piece, mastered the work, and brought the product to completion for you to enjoy.

Don't you sometimes wonder what you will look like as a finished product? Do you wonder, as I do, what God, the Master Artist, is making, shaping, and molding us to be? Don't you long to see the final product?

Aren't we grateful the product we now see is not the finished one?

He's still working on us! We are the clay, and he is the potter. Long ago, he conceived the idea of who we would be and has been fashioning us on his wheel to be a product we—and he—can enjoy, one that looks more and more like the potter himself!

We are clay … in his hands.

I've learned, after serving him for many years now, he does not work in a hurry. I've also learned much of his work is invisible. Oh, how I wish I could more easily see what he's doing, but that's just my impatience showing! He's working on that too.

I am his workmanship on the potter's wheel, and I am being changed. He is still working on me. The Creator of the universe—who spoke into existence an entire world and its expansive heavens—is working on me! What he is making out of my life is sure to be more than I've even dreamed possible, because he is able to do more than I could ever imagine.

In the potter's hands, I am being made beautiful.

He makes everything beautiful in its time.

—Ecclesiastes 3:11

For we are His workmanship, created in Christ Jesus for good works, which God prepared beforehand that we should walk in them.

—Ephesians 2:10

First, Not Finally

Trust in the Lord with all your heart,
And lean not on your own understanding.

—Proverbs 3:5

Far too often, I hear variations of this statement: "I've tried everything I know to do, and nothing is working, so now I'll give it to God (or now I just have to trust God)." When bad news comes, we are presented with a choice. We can give our concern to God first, with a heart full of trust; or we can try with everything we have in our own strength to solve the problem first, and eventually, after multiple failed efforts, give the situation to God. This choice to trust doesn't mean everything suddenly turns into sunshine and roses.

Circumstances do not instantly resolve themselves and fall perfectly into place. That's not how he works. Instead, we find our choice to trust God will bring a presence of peace we didn't have before. This is the kind of peace we read about in Isaiah 26:3: *You will keep him in perfect peace, whose mind is stayed on You, because he trusts in You.*

When I follow the pattern of *first* instead of *finally*, I am comforted. I know God is in control and trusting him allows me to approach every difficulty or stress with a much calmer state of mind. When I fall into the pattern of *finally* instead of *first*, I ultimately regret I didn't give my problem to God in the first place.

When will we learn to take everything to God, which is what we need to do *first* instead of *finally?*

Let's take our challenges to him in prayer.

"Lord, we give these situations to you; they are in your hands. You have the answers. We know you are with us, and we trust you with our life challenges. Please lead and guide us and grant us wisdom. We know these circumstances are not ours to handle alone. Amen."

Imperfect

Not that I have already attained, or am already perfected; but I press on, that I may lay hold of that for which Christ Jesus has also laid hold of me.

—Philippians 3:12

I met Karen, a new believer, for lunch one day. As we were talking, I realized she had the impression I was perfect, because I had been saved for a long time. I had casually mentioned a disagreement that occurred between my husband and me about finances before I'd left my house to meet her for lunch. I had said some harsh and unkind things to him. I told her about my feelings of guilt and how I needed to apologize as soon as I got home.

Karen surprised me by saying she was happy to know I was human, after all. As a new believer, much of our conversation had been about discipleship and teaching her about the Bible and what God's Word teaches us, and we hadn't yet moved to the practical side of life.

I'm glad our conversation steered us in that direction, because new believers need to know that those of us who have been walking with the Lord for a long time are not anywhere near perfect! We do get mad at our spouses and other people, we sometimes experience anger, and we are also sometimes guilty of harshness, unkindness, and other failings.

I'm glad she saw my imperfection. I think she was relieved to learn she didn't have to be perfect for God to continue loving her. We had a long talk about how God's Spirit, who indwells the believer, brings conviction when we do something wrong. The Holy Spirit convicts us to be sorry for our actions and apologize to the person we mistreated. This work of the Holy Spirit is why I wanted to apologize to my husband that day. Our discussion reminded us both that we truly are sinners, but we are saved by grace. Our desire is to be perfected, even though we aren't perfect, and to be more like Christ every day.

Yielded Heart

Show me Your ways, O LORD;
Teach me Your paths.
Lead me in Your truth and teach me,
For You are the God of my salvation;
On You I wait all the day.

—Psalm 25:4-5

Why is it so hard to surrender and yield to a high and Holy God, who is
our Abba Father?

YIELD: To relinquish control to someone or something; To give something
up to someone else; The opposite of being in control or in charge.

Although relinquishing control is hard, when we do yield, surrender
gives us a sweet reward of intimacy with the Lord. The relationship between
Father and child becomes knit together in strength, trust, and love. That's
when we learn to trust God's ways, not ours. That's how we tune our hearts
to an obedient walk and choose to press in close for all he has for us as he
leads and guides our lives. We gain much more than we lose when we give
our lives in total surrender to our heavenly Father and Lord.

There lies a constant risk of danger when we live unto ourselves and
our own ways, and not unto God and his ways. A life lived unto ourselves
becomes a painted target for Satan. Any part of our hearts not surrendered
to the Lord is the enemy's for the taking, and he will most certainly attack
those vulnerable places.

That's why giving ourselves completely to our God is so vitally
important, submitted and yielded, fully surrendering every part of our
hearts into his hands. The attacks still come when the enemy tempts us to
not trust God as he did with Eve in the garden, but God is our strength
and shield when we're yielded to him. He is the power that can overcome
anything the enemy brings against us—if our hearts are wholly surrendered
to him.

As believers, we are privileged to follow the Lord in our journey. By
faith and obedience, and because we love him and know we are loved
by him, we seek his ways, we draw close, and we keep our eyes on him.

We listen for his voice and we follow where he leads. Our yielded hearts understand a surrendered life is a life walked hand in hand with the Lord.

CHANGES

Being confident of this very thing, that He who has begun a good work in you will complete it until the day of Jesus Christ.

—Philippians 1:6

I am encouraged when I notice changes in myself and know God is slowly and steadily working in me. There have been times when I felt change would never come. I'm so thankful he is patient and loving, caring, and tenderhearted.

Through the process of changing me, molding me, and shaping me, he has never pushed, nor did he ever force me to change. Somehow, though, he made me want to be more like him. Over the passage of time his work in me produced a kinder more loving, more patient and forgiving person.

How glad I am that he continues to change me, and didn't leave me like I was five, ten, or even more years ago. I have no idea how he's done it, but, thankfully, I'm not that person anymore. His love and his life in me have reinvented me.

God keeps working out his plan for me as he works these changes in my life and in my heart. I am grateful he loves me enough to change me. Because he has given me a glimpse of what I can become, I know I want to be all he made me to be.

Emptied of me,
Filled with you.
You are changing me,
Molding me,
Making me
Who you want me to be.

Have I begun yet
To look a little more
Like you?

45

Surrendered

Open my eyes to see
The wonder of your ways.
Open my heart,

Surrendered,

That you may enter in.
Fill me up with all of you;
Leave nothing left of me,
Until in newness I can be
Who you made me to be,
All you want me to be.
I give to you my life,

Surrendered,

Reign over me.

CHAPTER THREE

Deep Abiding Love

You reached across the vast horizons,
Across the deep blue skies.
From heaven to earth you touched me,
And my life was changed
Forever
When you came into my heart.

Tenderly

Behold what manner of love the Father has bestowed on us, that we should be called children of God! Therefore the world does not know us, because it did not know Him.

—1 John 3:1

Beloved, let us love one another, for love is of God; and everyone who loves is born of God and knows God. He who does not love does not know God, for God is love.

—1 John 4:7-8

You hold my heart,
And tenderly
Your loving kindness far exceeds
All I ever thought was possible
From a high and Holy God.

But you are
FATHER.
You hold the greatest love of all
And freely offer it to me,
Tenderly.

God loves me—and you—with a love more tender than words can describe.

Many of us think of God as a stern and strict disciplinarian, rather than the caring and gentle heavenly Father he is. This often happens because we view him in the light of how our earthly fathers have treated us.

If you've had a good, loving father, then it's probably easier to see your Father God as good and loving. But he doesn't just have a loving side like our earthly fathers may have. *He is Love.* If you've had a stern and angry father or an abusive father, then it's easy to see God as a Father to be feared. When the Bible talks of fearing God, the words mean being in awe of him and respecting him for who he is. Scripture is not talking about the kind of fear we have of an earthly father who may be prone to anger and violence.

I grew up with an earthly father who was prone to anger and violence. And yet, because I know God, I view him as a tender and gentle, loving Father. I also know he is holy, almighty, all sovereign, and all powerful. I know that is who he is, and yet those characteristics don't strike fear in me. That's because this high and holy God comes to me—*with his love.*

He comes to me with love and with healing in his hands and frees me of a past I don't understand. *But I do know with all certainty my life was planned, he works things together for good, and he makes all things beautiful in his time.* I have definitely seen these things in my life, over and over again.

In those past things I don't understand, I can still see my Father holding me close in the palm of his hand. I always knew he loved me and I was never alone. In my heart, I always heard a voice tenderly calling my name. And the voice was … my FATHER'S voice.

Defining Moment: Part One

We love Him because He first loved us.

—1 John 4:19

Has there been a defining moment in your life when you *knew* that God loves you? *Really* loves you?

That defining moment for me came many years ago, when God showed me how much he loves and cares for me in a very special way. From that moment forward, I have never doubted his deep, abiding love for me.

I was single and in my early twenties in the summer of 1979 when I made a long road trip to visit a friend out of state. I was driving alone from Kentucky to Louisiana. There were no cell phones then.

I reached Nashville close to noon, and traffic was rather heavy. Because I was only passing through, I was driving in the far-left lane. Suddenly, my car started to lose power. I could tell it was dying! I frantically checked my mirrors and started changing lanes. As cars careened past me at a higher rate of speed, I steered into the far-right lane just as my car completely lost power. I coasted onto the shoulder of the highway.

How I was going to get help? How could I get to a place that could repair my car, and would I have enough money to pay for it? I was hundreds of miles from anyone who could come to my rescue, and my heart felt overwhelmed. I knew my only help would come from God. Somehow, he would have to show up and rescue me.

I closed my eyes, put my head on the steering wheel and cried out to the Lord in prayer. As I was saying the words, "Lord, help me," another driver had already pulled over to see if they could help. I whispered silently to the Lord, "I have to trust this person. You sent him, didn't you?"

The older gentleman who came to my aid told me he had a daughter my age. He told me if she had car trouble, he would want a compassionate person to stop and help her. He seemed kind and non-threatening. My heart filled with God's peace, and I thanked the man repeatedly for being that compassionate person who had stopped to help me. I also told him he was the answer to my prayer.

Amazingly, my car had coasted to a stop right before an exit where there was a gas station. The older man pushed my car with his, and with my car in neutral, we were able to get to the gas station. My car trouble turned out to be just a burned wire that needed replacing, and the gas station attendant only charged me $3.00!

The entire situation could not have turned out better for a young woman having car trouble far from home with very little money. I cried happy tears the rest of my trip. I had always known God loved me, but, in that moment, when he rescued me and took care of me the way he had, I knew his love in a deeper way than ever before. I also learned he knows where I am at any moment, because he is always with me.

When was your defining moment? What happened that helped you understand, without a doubt, that God really does love you?

Defining Moment Part Two: Love Defined

God was spelling out his love for me.
It is forever inscribed and embedded in my heart.

When my car broke down in Nashville, and God immediately came to my rescue, I learned both the depth and the width of his love for me. His love is deeper than I have ever known and is always with me, wherever I go, because he lives inside of me. Those lessons have become clearer and more precious to me with the passage of time. I grasped the truth of his love for me at a new level in that defining moment. As the years have passed by, I have gained an even deeper understanding and appreciation of the sheer magnitude of what he was teaching me all those years ago about his constant presence in my life and his protection and provision in times of need.

When you understand God's amazing love for you, you find such security that you no longer need to cling to a friend, your mate, a parent, or anyone else to find the love you are seeking. God's love removes your need to be co-dependent, which seems to be a prevalent challenge in our culture today. Our enemy, Satan, wants desperately for us to feel unloved, but we know the truth remains that we are the recipients of the greatest love on earth. Jesus died for us, and his immeasurable sacrifice should constantly fill us with the assurance of his love.

There will be times when you are alone and doubt the love of those around you. Remember God's love is everlasting and never ending. His love is always there for you. Believe with all of your heart, and his love will fill the emptiness left by the failing love of others. If you had an absent parent, whose love you never knew, God's love is enough. If you had a parent or spouse or sibling or child who was incapable of love, God's love is enough. If love is lacking in your life here on this earth, let God's love fill you, surround you, and carry you.

John 14:21 reminds us of the promise of God's love for us. *He who has My commandments and keeps them, it is he who loves Me. And he who loves Me will be loved by My Father, and I will love him and manifest Myself to him.*

Jesus loves me … and you … and He will continually reveal his love to us! *Now that is*

Love Defined!

Love Your Neighbor

Jesus said to him, "'You shall love the LORD your God with all your heart, with all your soul, and with all your mind.' This is the first and great commandment. And the second is like it: 'You shall love your neighbor as yourself.'"

—Matthew 22:37-39

God taught me a valuable lesson about loving our neighbors recently as I observed my husband's compassionate actions toward a lonely stranger. I was watering flowers on our front porch one evening, and Randy was doing yard work when an elderly woman we didn't recognize approached him and asked if we had seen her missing cat. She described the cat and my husband told her we hadn't seen it, but the woman continued to talk … and talk … and talk.

She told him she had been widowed for eight years, and she talked about the life she had shared with her husband that had spanned nearly half a century. She smiled as she told stories about their courting days, raising their family, and moving away from everyone she knew back east to follow his dream to live in the west. She talked about the many storms they had weathered together. The storm she was weathering most now, she said, was missing him.

She was lonely, and God provided a listening ear as my husband stood there and patiently listened, despite the darkening skies and the mosquitoes' bites. When she was done, we could tell by her changed countenance that she walked back to her home with a lighter step and cheerier heart.

Loving our neighbor as Jesus teaches should keep us sensitive to the heavy hearts around us that are burdened with a depth of loneliness we can help ease. All we need to do is show a bit of care and compassion. Sometimes, all we have to do is provide a listening ear.

Everlasting Love

The LORD has appeared of old to me, saying:
"Yes, I have loved you with an everlasting love;
Therefore with lovingkindness I have drawn you."
                                        —Jeremiah 31:3

Many years ago, when I was a young wife and mother, I sat down one day with my Bible and journal as I listened to Elisabeth Elliot speak on a Christian radio program. I was eager to take notes and learn more from a godly woman about the ways of the Lord and how to live the Christian life. She opened her program in that deep voice of hers and said, "You are loved with an everlasting love."

I wrote those words at the top of the page, and then I took diligent notes from her teaching that morning.

You are loved with an everlasting love.

The next day, I pulled out my journal and turned to the notes from the previous day as I began to listen to her program for the second time. I was surprised when she said those same stirring words at the beginning: "You are loved with an everlasting love." I wrote them down again. The next day, after I had heard her repeat the same words for a third morning in a row, I realized it must be her regular opening for her program every day, from the verse in Jeremiah 31:3.

I cherished that reminder every day of the qualities of God's everlasting love for us—unconditional, never failing, enduring, and full of compassion. Elisabeth Elliot understood the value in those words. As her gift to her listening audience, she proclaimed this great love God has for us in every one of her radio programs.

How thankful I am to know I am loved with his everlasting love. That love washes over me and fills me up every single day of my life.

Today, let me be the one to tell you …

You are loved with an everlasting love.

THE JUROR'S STORY

Casting all your care upon Him, for He cares for you.
—1 Peter 5:7

I've discovered God can use anything—even something as mundane as jury duty—to touch his people.

I served on a jury once with a woman named Laura. Laura was the quiet one who stayed behind when we broke at noon, and all the other jurors went scurrying off for lunch. As I, too, was walking out for lunch, I saw her sitting all alone at the big table in the meeting room, holding a brown paper bag. I asked if she wanted to join me for lunch, and she declined, pointing to her lunch sack. I told her I would just rush across the street and grab some food and come back and eat with her. After we ate, Laura began sharing with me she had recently broken through a time of depression. Her marriage—which she never dreamed would fall apart—had ended in divorce, and utter brokenness sent her into a deep valley of despair.

Laura didn't share the details of the divorce except to say her husband was the one who chose to leave. She said her greatest fear had been she would not be able to adequately take care of her children. She said fear began to consume her—fear of having to raise her children alone, fear of not being able to take care of everything around the house, and fear of being alone without a man in the home.

Eventually, the fear pervaded her life, causing her to spiral downward into depression. She was constantly afraid she would lose everything, just as she had lost her marriage. She shared she had been a born-again Christian for a long time, but when the divorce happened, she was so ashamed she stopped going to church. Ladies from her Bible study group had called to check on her, but she withdrew and wouldn't let them help her. One lady even stopped by with cookies and asked if she could come in and pray with her, but Laura had turned her away, saying, "Not today. I'm not up to it right now."

"God was right there all along," Laura said with a sigh, "offering me help and sending people who cared, and I just pushed them away because I let fear and shame take over my life." She was miserable being out of church, and yet too miserable to go back. Depression took its toll on her energy, causing increased difficulty to just get through her job each day and take care of her two young children. Her mother was able to help some. She also encouraged Laura to go back to church and be surrounded by people who would pray for, encourage, and support her.

Laura admitted she had dug in her heels and refused to take that step. She continued to feel worse, to the point of having trouble even getting out of bed and functioning each day. She called in sick one day and spent the entire day at home, just crying and praying. She knew she desperately needed help.

Laura slept better that night than she had in a long time. She went to work the next day with dark circles under her eyes from the day-long cry, but she felt a little better from having shed all those tears and having poured out her heart to God. As she walked from the parking lot to her office building, her heel caught on a scrap of paper. She removed the piece of paper and started to toss it in the trash, but something caught her attention, and she decided to read it first.

The paper was a brochure announcing a Bible study at an area church. The words that caught her attention in bold print across the top of the crumpled paper were *Cast all your care upon Him, because He cares for you* (1 Peter 5:7). She remembered her pastor preaching on the subject of giving your burdens to the Lord, but the topic hadn't meant anything to her when everything had been going well in her life. But that day, the words pierced her heart, and she suddenly felt a peace and comfort she had not known in months. The message that God cared for her broke through the wall of depression around her heart and flooded her with a new confidence that God would take care of her.

I listened, amazed, as she shared how God used that Bible verse to lift her out of her depression and how her life was changed by a single Scripture. I don't remember much about the case we heard as jurors that week, but I will always cherish the story I heard from Laura about how God brought her out of depression and gave her renewed hope for what the future held for her and her children.

God can—and will—do the same for you!

POURED OUT LOVE

Now hope does not disappoint, because the love of God has been poured out in our hearts by the Holy Spirit who was given to us.

—Romans 5:5

Fill a room with a group of women, ask them to open up and talk about their lives, their relationships, and their feelings, and sadly, you'll often find a room full of women with empty, broken hearts. I've been in that room and I have felt the emptiness many women feel. This plague of emptiness shouldn't be that way.

In most of their personal life stories, the pain of life had caused a disconnection to occur. That kind of disconnect blinds a hurting person to the hope of God's love and to the healing his love brings. And my heart breaks as I long for their eyes to see the depth of God's love—a love they've somehow missed.

There is hope for every heart. When those empty hearts are invaded with the unending, unfailing, everlasting love of God, they are filled higher than they have ever been filled before. You can know God's love exists and that he loves you—even better is to *experience the fullness of life* that comes when God's love is pouring into your heart and flowing like a river—a river of life.

Many women experience rejection and loneliness. They live with the hurt of a failed relationship or they're longing to find a relationship that will fill them with love. Even some people who are in good, loving marriages find themselves longing for a deeper love. But marriage and family relationships can't fulfill that longing, because the only love that fully satisfies is God's love. God's love makes an empty heart full and a broken heart whole.

Only God's love takes away the emptiness. Only God's love loves enough. Only God's love can.

LOVED LIKE THIS

> For I am persuaded that neither death nor life, nor angels nor principalities nor powers, nor things present nor things to come, nor height nor depth, nor any other created thing, shall be able to separate us from the love of God which is in Christ Jesus our Lord.
>
> —Romans 8:38-39

Experiencing the *permanent, lasting* love this passage describes can make our worries and troubles seem small, especially when we look back and compare them to the life we lived before we knew God's love. When I start to worry, I remind myself I'm God's child and I'm loved. Then I feel the comforting blanket of his amazing love and peace surrounding me. Oh, how glad I am that I'm loved like this!

The woman at the well in the fourth chapter of John had spent her life looking for that kind of lasting love in all the wrong places—through relationships with six men. Then Jesus offered her the fountain of his perfect love, the living water that really satisfies. Our misguided tendencies to look for satisfaction in the expectations and conditions others put before us only leads to death. Drinking from the fullness of God's love is a far better way to live, as it produces *life*.

When the love of others is broken and frail, you can count on a love that always satisfies and never fails—God's love. Is your heart filled to overflowing with his love? Aren't you forever grateful as I am that his is a love that loves enough?

> Jesus answered and said to her, "Whoever drinks of this water will thirst again, but whoever drinks of the water that I shall give him will never thirst. But the water that I shall give him will become in him a fountain of water springing up into everlasting life."
>
> —John 4:13-14

THE PRODIGAL'S RETURN

> But the father said to his servants, "Bring out the best robe and put it on him, and put a ring on his hand and sandals on his feet. And bring the fatted calf here and kill it, and let us eat and be merry; for this my son was dead and is alive again; he was lost and is found." And they began to be merry.
> —Luke 15:22-24

If you ever find yourself wondering what kind of reunion God plans for his children who stray and then come home, read the story in Luke 15 about the prodigal son. The young son demanded his share of the inheritance and left home to live a life of sin that took him down a path of destruction so disastrous he finally decided to go home again. Upon his return, his father lovingly, eagerly, fully accepted him.

One of the most beautiful aspects of this parable is the father did not place his focus on what the wayward son had done, or how far he had fallen. Instead, the loving father placed his full focus on his wayward son's return.

The prodigal son admitted his wrong ways, confessed his sin, repented, and returned to his home. But his expectations of his father were very low. He expected to be received back, not as his son, but as a hired servant. This prodigal son must have been overwhelmed by the reunion when he returned, for he was fully accepted, fully restored, and shown his father's unfailing love.

We see in this story that the adult child who strayed and walked a path of destruction was completely restored. His return gave the father great cause to rejoice and celebrate.

You see, the father had longingly waited the entire time for his son to come home. After all, the wayward son was his child, and he had never stopped loving him. Just as the loving father in this story gladly, joyfully, gave so much in fully restoring his son to the family, our Abba Father gave the ultimate gift—the sacrificial death of his own son—to fully restore us, his children, to his family. He, along with all the angels in heaven, rejoices when we return home. We were lost, but now we're found. What a great cause to be merry!

Never Unworthy

For You formed my inward parts;
You covered me in my mother's womb.
I will praise You, for I am fearfully and wonderfully made;
Marvelous are Your works,
And that my soul knows very well.
My frame was not hidden from You,
When I was made in secret,
And skillfully wrought in the lowest parts of the earth.
Your eyes saw my substance, being yet unformed.
And in Your book they all were written,
The days fashioned for me,
When as yet there were none of them.

—Psalm 139:13-16

How do you feel about yourself? Do you know how valuable you are?

When I hear someone say they don't like themselves or they think they are unworthy, I quickly speak up. For too long, Satan has successfully used that tactic to drag people away from the truth of their own worthiness to God.

God made you and God loves you, and those two facts are powerful truths you can hold onto when you begin to have feelings of unworthiness. The devil delights in making you believe you are unworthy—a lie he uses to detour and deceive you from seeing yourself as God sees you.

When you see yourself as God sees you, and when you understand he loves you with an unconditional love that far surpasses any human love you could receive on this earth, only then will you feel worthy.

He loves you! He made you! He formed you with a unique and special design and made a special plan for your life!

The enemy will do everything he can to make you not believe this. Satan wants to destroy people. He has many tactics that he uses over and over. He wants to distort your image of yourself into something that is not at all how God sees you. His objective is to make you feel unloved and unworthy.

But you are not, and you will never be, unworthy to God. God wants you to trust him and believe in his great love for you. Trust and believe in the worth and value he places on your life, a life he planned.

THE NOTE CARD

For God so loved the world that He gave His only begotten Son, that whoever believes in Him should not perish but have everlasting life.

—John 3:16

She forgot God loved her, but God did not forget her.

Several years ago, as we left to go on a family trip to visit my husband's parents, I left a note in our mailbox asking the mail carrier to hold our mail that week. The note card I selected from my stationery pile had the verse John 3:16 written across the front. I wrote my note inside, politely giving her the dates to hold our mail. A few weeks later, as I was doing yard work in our front yard, the mail carrier stopped at our mailbox and called out that she wanted to tell me something. As I walked to the end of the driveway, I could see was excited. She had a huge smile on her face, and she was literally beaming. She told me she was so glad I was out in the yard because she wanted to thank me for the card. Then she shared something I will never forget.

She had been a Christian for a long time, but after surviving a bitter divorce, she had run as far from God as she could. She constantly felt unworthy of his love. Family and friends had prayed for her and told her God still loved her, but she felt a million miles away from him ... until the day she pulled up to our mailbox and pulled out the note card bearing the words of John 3:16: *For God so loved the world that He gave His only begotten Son, that whoever believes in Him should not perish but have everlasting life.* She said the words on the note card proclaiming God's immeasurable love penetrated the wall around her heavy heart and brought her back to her heavenly Father, and she had been celebrating their renewed relationship ever since that day. She had taken the card home and tucked it into the edge of her mirror as a daily reminder of God's love for her. She couldn't wait to tell me, wishing every day I would be outside when she came by to deliver the mail.

I had always thought of John 3:16 as a verse to bring lost people to salvation in the Lord. I learned that day that sometimes the verse brings believers who find themselves feeling lost, alone, and unloved back to the Lord because the words remind them of the amazing love he has for all of us!

This story also amazes me because of the demonstration of the power of prayer. The mail carrier's family and friends had been praying for her to come back to the Lord, and for healing from her hurt. God used a stranger her friends and family would never meet to put a note card in her mailbox that would answer their prayers. A simple note card containing the most meaningful verse in the Bible broke through the wall of hurt around her heart, and God's love suddenly came rushing back in. The healing for which her family and friends had prayed happened instantly. She came back to God and into a close relationship with him, and she found a depth of love and acceptance only God can give. She found healing and wholeness in the power of the beloved, inspired words of John 3:16.

How is your heart, child of God? Do you need to be reminded of that powerful verse? It's the epitome of truth, you know: *For God so loved the world that He gave His only begotten Son, that whoever believes in Him should not perish but have everlasting life.* "Whoever" includes you.

ALWAYS LOVED

The Lord has appeared of old to me, saying:
"Yes, I have loved you with an everlasting love;
Therefore with lovingkindness I have drawn you."
—Jeremiah 31:3

Why do I sometimes have days when I feel so far from God's love? *Are you still there, Lord? When I can't seem to feel anything at all, then start to feel unworthy,* **are you still there?** *I know the feelings I am experiencing are not based on your truth, and I know my feelings are not the measure of your love for me.*

On these days all I want is reassurance that you're still here for me—still loving me—and I ask again ...

Lord, please...
Wrap me tighter in your love.
Stop the world from pressing in;
Stop the world from darkening my eyes
To see your truth.

Let my eyes see only you;
Then my heart will always know,
There is a love that holds me
In your loving, warm embrace.

In this world there is a constant force—a constant pressure, if you will—pushing in and trying to diminish the truth of God's amazing love for us. There is a spiritual warfare occurring that strives to make us doubt we are loved by our heavenly Father. Why should it surprise us that this would take place in a world where we have an enemy who is only after our destruction?

The truth we know and acknowledge in our own hearts will overcome the enemy's lies. We are loved with an everlasting love. We are loved with the greatest love in the whole world. How do we know? The Bible tells us so.

How grateful we can be that on those days when we feel unlovable we can still know we are worthy, and we are loved by a steadfast, immeasurable love.

You are still there.

For I am persuaded that neither death nor life, nor angels nor principalities nor powers, nor things present nor things to come, nor height nor depth, nor any other created thing, shall be able to separate us from the love of God which is in Christ Jesus our Lord.

—Romans 8:38-39

IN THE CHECKOUT LINE

"You are the salt of the earth; but if the salt loses its flavor, how shall it be seasoned? It is then good for nothing but to be thrown out and trampled underfoot by men. You are the light of the world. A city that is set on a hill cannot be hidden. Nor do they light a lamp and put it under a basket, but on a lampstand, and it gives light to all who are in the house. Let your light so shine before men, that they may see your good works and glorify your Father in heaven."

—Matthew 5:13-16

I try to be friendly to the checkout clerks at the grocery store. I may not directly share the gospel with them, but I can smile and be a friendly face and voice, and maybe the light of Jesus will shine through me … I hope.

I tend to ramble and have probably made a few people in line behind me wish I would be quiet and hurry on. If there's a substantial line, I try to rein myself in. But being friendly is important to me. I try to be graceful. Sometimes I do better than other times.

One time, I was talking to a young man who was scanning my items at the grocery store, and I went off on a rabbit trail. For some reason, I mentioned I would be making tuna sandwiches for lunch for my husband that day. It was a Saturday in the summertime, when I often made tuna or salmon sandwiches for lunch. I remember thinking how silly I sounded and realized I was rambling too much … again.

But the young man stopped and looked directly at me with a very serious look.

He said, "I wish I had someone who would make tuna sandwiches for me."

I saw loneliness.

I saw an ache and a longing.

I could hear his heart saying he wanted someone to love him.

In the look on that young face, I suddenly knew why I had said what I said.

I may not have shared the *gospel* of Christ with him, but, simply by talking to him and being friendly, I shared the *love* of Christ, right there in the checkout line. Maybe it's better said this way: *You can shine the light of Christ, even in the checkout line.*

His response reminded me to keep doing what I was doing. As I walked away, I realized it's not necessarily what you say as much as that you say something. People are lonely, hurting, longing.

They want to be noticed and heard. They want to be engaged … even in a brief conversation in the checkout line.

We can do that, because we are salt and light in this world.

The Same Amazing Love

The effective, fervent prayer of a righteous man avails much.
—James 5:16b

When It Is Difficult to Love—Keep Praying, Keep Loving

Have you ever prayed for someone's salvation for years and wondered if your prayers would ever be answered? I have. After years of investing prayer on someone's behalf, the person has continually pushed people away who try to come close and show they care. In fact, the best way to describe this person is to think of a prickly cactus or porcupine—definitely someone who doesn't welcome a warm, caring hug.

As I prayed for this lost person recently, I asked God again to do a work in his heart to convict him of his need for Christ. I immediately recognized God doing a convicting work in my own heart. He asked me to demonstrate love to this person in a way I had never done before. I realized God wanted me to show this person the same amazing love he has shown me. The hope is, as this person visibly sees God's love flowing from me, maybe he will see my love is the same amazing love God has for him.

Since then, I have been making that effort and reaching out in ways I had not done before. I have not yet noticed any change, but I believe God is doing a work I cannot see. The results are not up to me, but obedience to follow God's leading in my life *is* up to me. God continues to remind me to pray for this person and to demonstrate the love of Jesus Christ.

I have seen God's love break through the barriers other people have put around their hearts and have watched his love penetrate the walls, the cactus prickles, and the porcupine quills they've used to protect themselves. I believe, as I continue to love this hard-to-love person day by day, the barriers will begin to crack and crumble, and his heart will someday be exposed and open to receiving God's amazing love.

For this, I will continue to pray.

Will They See You in Me?

When people look at me,
Will they see you?
When people talk to me,
Will they hear you?

When people come to me,
And need the strength
That you can give,
Will I show them
You're the one,
The only one they need?

If I'm your hands and feet,
Will others know?
If I reach out with love,
Will they know it comes from you?

If I step out and show the love,
That you have shown to me
Will they come to you,
Wanting what they've seen in me,
Wishing for the same?

If they see you in me
Will they come?
Will they want to know you, Lord
If they see you in me?

CHAPTER FOUR

FAITH'S JOURNEY

God sees the things

I cannot see,

But I see him

And I believe.

In God I Trust

Trust in the Lord with all your heart,
And lean not on your own understanding;
In all your ways acknowledge Him,
And He shall direct your paths.

—Proverbs 3:5-6

My life verses are Proverbs 3:5-6. Life verses are those favored verses that hold a deep meaning to us, personally. They are the verses we go to most often to help guide our lives.

When I am faced with choices, struggles, and uncertainties, these verses in Proverbs are the ones I run to. These are the verses I know will help me with any situation in my life.

Trust in the Lord with all your heart. Trust is vital. Trust is faith in action. Trust is the essence of faith and the essence of my walk—my relationship—with God. God has built trust deep into my being, and trust lies at the core of how I live my life. God supplies the trust (faith), but I must be the one who acts.

And lean not on your own understanding. We need to understand that *when we are in a trusting relationship with God,* we cannot go through life doing things our own way. We will have a divided heart if we try. I learned a valuable lesson when I learned to just let go of my own way and go his way. It's really not complicated. *My heavenly Father knows best.*

In all your ways acknowledge Him. Believe God is who he says he is and make him Lord of your life. See his holiness. See his majesty and power. See every knee bowed low before him one day. He is God. He is in control. He is sovereign.

And He shall direct your paths. My life is in his hands. As I follow him, I'm going where he is leading; that's how I know I am where I am supposed to be and going where I am supposed to be going. Even the twists and turns in my path are being sovereignly navigated by God as I yield my heart and life to his will. I've trusted him with all my heart, I've not leaned on my own understanding, and I've acknowledged him in all my ways. Therefore, I know he is directing my paths.

There is power to live the Christian life in these two amazing verses. As you read these familiar verses again today, I pray they plant themselves deep in your heart and grow an unshakable and lasting trust in the Lord your God.

What Faith Looks Like—A Choice to Trust

I will say of the LORD, "He is my refuge and my fortress;
My God, in Him I will trust."

—Psalm 91:2

As we walk with the Lord in this journey of faith, what does walking by faith look like? Sometimes our walk looks like a thousand questions to which there are no answers, leaving us wondering what in the world is going on. We might ask, "How can things be so messed up? How can everything be fixed? Will it ever be straightened out?"

I've learned I have a choice. In fact, I have a significant choice:

Trust the Lord. Trust the sovereign, holy, Almighty God.

This choice brings me peace—a peace that cannot be explained, because the assurance comes in the midst of the thousand questions and troubling circumstances that still need to be untangled.

In this journey of faith, what does faith look like? *Faith looks like a choice to trust God.* That's not a cliché—a strong faith that trusts, no matter what the circumstances are.

If I don't make this choice, then what is the alternative? Trying to control circumstances I cannot control, and fighting worry, anxiety, anger, fear, and the list goes on.

What if I made two lists? The first list would be "Things I Understand, Things I Can Control, and Things I Can Fix." The second list would be "Things I Don't Understand, Things I Can't Control, and Things I Cannot Fix." Which list would be longer? Obviously, I think we'd all agree, the longer list would be the list of things I cannot control, cannot fix, and cannot understand.

Oh, but there is a third list I could make called: "Why I Choose My Faith and Choose to Trust in God." What would be on that list? "My history with God, and all he's already done for me." And under that I would list:

"He saved me. He loves me. He daily pours grace and mercy into my life. He's already worked in a thousand amazing ways in my life, which have all taught me who he is and that I can trust him. He has strengthened my faith in a life-long journey, and he calls me to this faith with every unanswered question, with every situation that is out of my control."

Faith is the answer to a thousand unanswered questions, and it happens in the choice to fully place our trust in the Lord.

Can't Explain It

The Lord is my rock and my fortress and my deliverer;
My God, my strength, in whom I will trust;
My shield and the horn of my salvation, my stronghold.
—Psalm 18:2

If I could explain all of life's mysteries, I wouldn't need to live by faith. If I could answer all my own questions, where would be the need for trust? If life came with a road map, why would I need to follow God? I want answers and solutions, but God wants me to trust him with all my heart.

Trust in the LORD with all your heart, and lean not on your own understanding; In all your ways acknowledge Him, and He shall direct your paths.
—Proverbs 3:5-6

When I feel anxious and stressed due to life's uncertainties, frustrations, and my own inability to grasp understanding about a troubling circumstance, I always remind myself of Proverbs 3:5-6. (It's my life verse, remember?) But there is also great treasure in verses 7 and 8, as they go on to remind us *Do not be wise in your own eyes; fear the Lord and depart from evil. It will be health to your flesh and strength to your bones.* This whole passage in Proverbs has brought me peace of mind more times than I can count. My heart is grateful for the comfort these powerful and wise words deliver.

I can't explain why things happen in life the way they do. I will be the first to admit that I want answers and solutions just like everyone else, but I also know that God wants me to trust him with all my heart instead of fretting over the solutions. We are tested more than we want to be by the hard times we go through and the questions that challenge us. Yet, if we want to pass the test, let us focus first on our hearts.

Are our hearts fully surrendered to the Lord?

There will be times when God is silent and trusting him completely during those times requires a huge leap of faith. And that's exactly what God is growing in us during those times—a fuller, deeper faith. We need to understand God's silence does not mean he is absent. He will never leave us or forsake us. God's silence is simply his asking us to have faith and teaching us to wait on him.

God's silence calls us to live by faith.

Just a Jar of Oil

And my God shall supply all your need according to His riches
in glory by Christ Jesus.

—Philippians 4:19

You may be familiar with the story of the prophet Elisha and the
widow's oil in 2 Kings 4:1-7. Recently, I reread this amazing story, and I
found myself visualizing the bottle of olive oil I have in my pantry. Then
I imagined pulling out all of the empty jars I store in my kitchen and
thought about pouring my bottle of extra virgin olive oil into one of those
jars, and then into a second jar, and then a third, and a fourth, and so on.
How awesome to see that kind of miracle happen before my eyes!

I haven't been in the same kind of dire situation as the widow we are
told about in 2 Kings 4. Creditors were threatening to take this widow's
two sons for slaves if she didn't pay her debt. The prophet Elisha asked her
what she had, and she responded that she had nothing in the house but
just a jar of oil.

As the story goes on, Elisha told her to borrow empty vessels from her
neighbors—as many as she could get. She collected many vessels and filled
every one of them with the oil from her one jar. Then she sold the oil.
The payoff was enough to take care of her debt and thus secure her sons'
freedom, with enough left over to provide for her and her sons for the rest
of her days. God definitely intervened with a miracle of multiplication
in this story, as he turned her one jar of oil into enough to fill numerous
empty vessels.

This great story from the Old Testament is one of many that teach us
to trust our God to provide. The illustration teaches us to believe he will
meet our needs. God's provision for this widow rose far above and beyond
her immediate need to pay a debt to prevent her sons from being sold into
slavery.

If God can use *just a jar of oil* to pay off the widow's debt and provide
enough remaining funds to take care of her family, then we should be
encouraged that he is capable of multiplying what we have or providing
what we need in ways we have not thought possible.

So, the next time you pull out your bottle of olive oil from your kitchen pantry, remember what God did for this widow woman and her two sons. Believe that he is still in the business of meeting our needs above and beyond all we can comprehend and in ways we could not have imagined.

> Now to Him who is able to do exceedingly abundantly above all that we ask or think, according to the power that works in us, to Him be glory in the church by Christ Jesus to all generations, forever and ever. Amen.
>
> —Ephesians 3:20-21

The Fabric of My Faith

But without faith it is impossible to please Him, for he who comes to God must believe that He is, and that He is a rewarder of those who diligently seek Him.

—Hebrews 11:6

Faith is woven throughout the everyday fabric of my life—in the big and small circumstances; in the hard and perplexing uncertainties; in the overwhelming gigantic trials that descend upon me; and in the quiet moments when God is calling my name, drawing me near, and asking me to follow wherever he leads. I will choose faith because this is what God desires.

God wants us to have *Faith;*

He wants us to *Trust;*

He wants us to *Believe;*

He requires that we *wait patiently on Him.*

All of this works with our obedience in following God, and our obedience in following him in what he has called us to do—which is his purpose in us!

We will accomplish more through our faith than through anything else—works, abilities, talents, or degrees. Our faith is the outward demonstration of a heart that completely trusts God and believes he will do for us and through us what we cannot do in our own strength.

David could not kill Goliath in his own strength. That was God's power in the slingshot and behind the stone that hit Goliath. The faith was David's, but the power was God's.

Joshua and his army could not make the wall of Jericho fall down with their shouting and trumpets, but they demonstrated faith and obedience—

and God, in his power, brought down an entire city wall in the blink of an eye.

To get through every day takes faith, as each day comes with challenges that force us to choose. Will we live by faith and trust in God? Or will we choose the alternative—trust in ourselves and the world around us? Some days bring challenges that rise up like giants before us. Do we dare believe that God will defeat the giants for us? To believe he will takes faith, and I want to be counted faithful. Don't you?

> And I thank Christ Jesus our Lord who has enabled me, because He counted me faithful, putting me into the ministry.
> —1 Timothy 1:12

Manna Faith

> But seek first the kingdom of God and His righteousness, and all these things shall be added to you. Therefore do not worry about tomorrow, for tomorrow will worry about its own things. Sufficient for the day is its own trouble.
>
> —Matthew 6:33-34

Do you marvel, as I do, at God's miraculous and incredible provision for the Israelites' journey in the wilderness? He provided their daily supply of manna from heaven (Exodus 16) in the precise amount that was needed, one day at a time!

That's what God does for us, you know. Living by faith, one day at a time, is our manna as we go through our wilderness experience. Just as the Lord gave the Israelites manna from heaven every day, he gives us precisely what we need for each day and for that one day alone. Faith recognizes we have been given exactly what we need today—and faith believes that tomorrow, God will do the same. Tomorrow, he will meet every need for that day. What we trusted him for today and received, we can trust him for again tomorrow.

Maybe we need a provision of food or clothes or money to pay the bills. *Maybe a vehicle.*

A few years ago, we gave away our second vehicle to a missionary who was in great need of a car. His work was in the US, and he traveled much of the time. When our pastor announced this missionary's need, my husband knew God was telling him to give the missionary one of our cars. We discussed the donation, and I agreed.

We didn't know exactly how we would manage without our second car or how long raising the funds towards the purchase of a replacement vehicle would take. We did trust God to meet our need. Remarkably, not long after, we were given a vehicle by a family member who could no longer drive.

God met the need of the missionary and our need to replace the car we gave away! This was a double manna faith blessing!

Let the Winds Blow

The wind blows where it wishes, and you hear the sound of it,
but cannot tell where it comes from and where it goes. So is
everyone who is born of the Spirit.

—John 3:8

Every day of the first week of September 2012, the temperature was
over one hundred degrees. On a Friday afternoon at three p.m., the
thermometer read one hundred four degrees, breaking the previous heat
record for this day in North Texas.

Later that evening, my husband attended a high school football game
in Denton, which is farther north than where we live in the Dallas area.
He texted me at nine p.m. "North wind beginning to blow." At 9:10 p.m.
"Serious wind blowing now." *Let the winds blow.*

I thought I might have heard a little wind. Maybe, just maybe, the
predicted cool front was at my back door. I stepped outside to see if we
were experiencing any change yet at home. Instead, I was greeted with the
same stifling hot air as with each previous check. It was ninety-two at nine
p.m. *Let the winds blow.*

But an hour later, I knew the front was at my back door because I could
hear powerful, gusting winds. The reprieve from a long, hot summer had
arrived, and you could hear a city breathe in relief. The north winds were
blowing, and we gladly said goodbye to the record-breaking heat of an
entire week. *Let the winds blow.*

I couldn't see that wind, but I could certainly feel the effects. The
mysterious line between visible and invisible revealed the evidence of the
unseen wind. My hair whipping around my face definitely felt the effects as
I stood in the back yard welcoming the north wind and the cooler weather
being ushered in. Although dark, in the shadows of the night I could see
tree branches and leaves blowing in the strong wind and other plants and
flowers bent over by the force. *Let the winds blow.*

There is a greater invisible mystery, and that is our invisible God. I can't
see God, but I feel his effects. His life and his Spirit have been breathed

into me. He has changed me. His work in my life is like the wind that I can't see, but I know he's there, doing an invisible work.

Yes! I believe in a God I can't see. I believe in the salvation that is mine because I accept his free gift of eternal life by grace through faith in his Son, Jesus Christ. I believe in the invisible regenerating work he did that made me a new creation. There are a lot of unseen factors in this Christian walk as the evidence of an unseen God is lived out in my life every day. The effects of God in my life are just as real as the autumn winds beginning to blow across the plains of Texas. Our Christian walk is called a life of faith. *Let the winds blow!*

Faith Sees Me Through

I will instruct you and teach you in the way you should go;
I will guide you with my eye.

—Psalm 32:8

Today, I whispered to the Lord,
"I want to do what you want me to do,
Even when I don't know what that is.
Lord, I will go where you want me to go,
Even when I don't know where."

There have been times I have not known precisely what God has for me. Ours is a journey of discovery—a faith journey.

There are times I put one foot in front of the other, not even knowing with any certainty, especially in my writing journey, where I am going or if I am even going in the right direction. I just keep praying, "God lead me, guide me, show me the way you have for me to go. Show me your ways!"

As I take blind steps in my journey, *faith sees me through,* one day at a time. Living by faith happens one single step at a time—and though I don't always know where I am going, I know who I am following! This is how I know I am going exactly where he is leading me.

"For as the heavens are higher than the earth,
So are My ways higher than your ways,
And My thoughts than your thoughts."

—Isaiah 55:9

I have learned that I cannot expect to know or understand many aspects of the faith journey. If I did, I wouldn't be on a faith journey at all. His ways and thoughts are higher than mine. Why would I question them? *If I could figure life all out on my own, then where is the faith in that?*

I have also learned that the faith journey is a journey of yielding, submitting, and surrendering. *After all, who is in control of my life—me or God? Who has the master plan—me or the Master?*

A Door for Hope

Hope deferred makes the heart sick,
But when the desire comes, it is a tree of life.
—Proverbs 13:12

During my time of prayer one morning, I reviewed the names and requests in my prayer journal and found a name that made me stop to consider who else was praying for the needs of this person. I made a sad conclusion. Recalling recent conversations with relatives and friends, I realized most of them had given up on this person. I had often faced discouragement myself as the years slipped by without any change, without any apparent softening of his heart toward the message of God's love and his gift of salvation through faith in his Son, Jesus Christ.

Many of us have been praying for a loved one on our prayer list for a long time. Maybe the name on your list is someone who has turned away from the Lord, and you have diligently prayed for this prodigal son or daughter to come home. Maybe the name on your list is a relative or friend who has never called upon the Lord for salvation, and you have prayed for this loved one for many years, but still have not seen this prayer answered. You can easily think that because there has been no change after all this time, there never will be. That attitude can lead to our giving up praying for them.

Sometimes, we become discouraged when answers don't appear. It is hard to understand when we pray for someone and don't see anything happen year after year after year. Even when we are discouraged and weary, we must continue in diligent prayer and keep believing God is doing a work we cannot see—yet. We must never give up, and instead, always leave open a door for hope! Ask God to give you more love and compassion for those on your prayer list. As you keep praying for their return to the Lord or their salvation, may you see that your prayers always keep open ... a door for hope.

THE WAITING SIDE OF FAITH

Wait on the LORD;
Be of good courage,
And He shall strengthen your heart;
Wait, I say, on the LORD!

—Psalm 27:14

Our Christian walk of faith is often a journey of waiting ... and waiting. We don't always do that waiting with much patience. You can put my name at the top of that list, but I am learning. Waiting is hard, because we don't know what the answer will be. Neither do we know when the answer will come. Yet, knowing that God holds the answer turns our waiting into *trust*. As a result, faith renews our strength to wait. And we will need a lot of strength, because we will do a great deal of waiting on our faith journey.

Everything we do, we do by faith. As faith is enabling us to trust and wait, it is also building more faith to help us wait on him for the results. Many times, those results are a long, long time coming. Yet, faith is required day by day for the journey. Our journey isn't necessarily about the end result, but how we endure the unknown.

Will we endure when we grow discouraged when we don't see improvement in a loved one's illness? Will we trust him to renew our strength and move us out of the place of discouragement to a place of peace and hope again when a difficult family relationship shows no signs of improving yet? In my experience, when I call out to him with my discouraged heart, he is always faithful to lift me up again; then I can rest once again in knowing he is in control.

Faith is often a *waiting journey*.
Faith is not a walk of knowing.
Faith is not a knowing journey.
Faith is knowing him;
Not knowing what the future holds,
But knowing the one who holds the future,
Knowing he is God,
Knowing he is Sovereign.

The choice to trust will help us wait. This choice will help us persevere and endure and grow and learn. It will test us and teach us, and our faith will grow deeper. A deeper faith is the result of steadfastly waiting on the Lord.

Pray Before You Leap

Be anxious for nothing, but in everything by prayer and supplication, with thanksgiving, let your requests be made known to God; and the peace of God, which surpasses all understanding, will guard your hearts and minds through Christ Jesus.

—Philippians 4:6-7

When I was in my early twenties, I moved without even praying about relocating. I loved God, and I did not intend to go the wrong way. But, I had not yet learned we are to seek God as we make choices and decisions. I simply plowed ahead, completely tossing all wisdom aside.

I was a young Christian and hadn't read my Bible much or heard a lot of teaching, so I didn't know to even pray about choices and decisions. I had not been raised in the church and had not learned these important spiritual lessons.

I immaturely quit my job and moved out of state, simply because I was not satisfied with the status quo. Long story short, that move failed miserably, and I ended up back in the same town, but without an apartment, furniture, or a job. I had to start completely over.

But not long after, the man I would marry came into the picture, and I knew exactly why God brought me back.

When I saw what God had done by reversing my bad decision and bringing me back, and how he'd brought my husband across my path by moving him to my town and bringing him to my church, God's grace and love for me were forged deeply across my heart forever.

Oh, I am grateful he covers us with a lot of tender grace in our youth and that he is patient with us as we learn and grow in the ways of the Lord.

God definitely caught my attention through that experience, as I saw him work in my life in such an amazing way. Those events were a significant turning point in my spiritual growth, and the experience impacted the depth of faith I walk in today.

God cares about every detail of our lives, and he has a plan that is slowly unfolding through the circumstances we experience, including our own unwise and immature choices. We would be wise to seek him and pray, and also to trust and wait on him.

Faith That Grows

And my God shall supply all your need according to His riches
in glory by Christ Jesus.

—Philippians 4:19

There was a lady, Melinda, in my Sunday school class years ago whose
ex-husband was in jail. She was severely struggling financially to provide
for her two sons. I watched Melinda also struggle with her faith to trust
God to take care of her and meet the needs for her sons.

I often encouraged her, because I sincerely believed God would meet
her needs and provide for her and her two boys. She would tell me she
wanted to trust God, but the whole situation looked so impossible.

One Sunday, she came in especially discouraged because a car repair had
emptied out her checkbook, and she desperately needed groceries. What
she didn't know was that our Sunday school class had already decided to
fill her pantry, and every lady in our class had brought in a bag of groceries
that morning. They were hidden in the classroom closet. The joy on her
face was priceless when we surprised her with this blessing of groceries, and
she saw what we had done for her family.

We saw her faith begin to grow after that. She still struggled, but now
she would say, "I know God will provide!"

At Christmas, Melinda worried she wouldn't be able to buy any presents
for her boys, but what she didn't know was several men in our church
had collected money to buy two bikes and other gifts for her young sons.
Melinda was right. She didn't have enough money to buy gifts that year.
But she didn't have to because they were bought by others in our church
who knew she was in a difficult situation and wanted her boys to have a
good Christmas.

When I urge someone to trust God and to have faith that he will see
them through a difficult circumstance, I'm not just speaking empty words.
They are words to live by. I've seen God grow my own faith, which has
helped me trust in him throughout the days and years of my life, and
because I have witnessed his action in the lives of others who have also seen
God work in amazing ways to demonstrate his loving care for them.

GOD MOVES FOR US

> But without faith it is impossible to please Him, for he who comes to God must believe that He is, and that He is a rewarder of those who diligently seek Him.
>
> —Hebrews 11:6

As I've been learning to walk by faith and obedience in my relationship with God, I have found many examples from people in the Bible. These people exemplify what happens *when we make a move of faith—God then moves for us*. What do I mean by that? When we answer a call to faith and step out and make a move to demonstrate our faith, then God *shows up*. And when he moves, he does the *supernatural*.

In Joshua 6, Joshua and the Israelites faithfully and obediently marched around the Jericho wall shouting and blowing their trumpets, and then the wall fell flat just as God. The wall wide enough for two chariots to pass on its top, fell flat. No one blew it up—they simply blew trumpets and God did the rest.

In 1 Samuel 17, David took a slingshot and five stones to defeat a mighty giant. God sent David's first stone in a deadly hurl straight into Goliath's head. David didn't have a super bionic arm. He had faith in an all-powerful God.

In Judges 7, Gideon had originally obeyed God's directive and started with an army of thirty-two thousand, but then God said, *tell the ones who are afraid that they may leave*, and the numbers quickly dropped to ten thousand. Then God said, *that's still too many*, and he dropped the numbers again to three hundred with a water-lapping test. With these three hundred remaining men, the battle was won—with trumpets, pitchers, and torches, not traditional weapons of war.

These are only a few instances of many we read in the Bible, but the lesson is clear in all of them. Faith and obedience please God, and then God moves for us! A demonstration of faith will produce a God-sized result, and a God-sized result is greater than anything we could do on our own.

When we are facing monumental situations in our lives, these examples from Scripture remind us to stand firm in our faith, walk diligently in obedience, and fully trust that God is going to move on our behalf.

UNSHAKEN

I have set the LORD always before me;
Because He is at my right hand I shall not be moved.

—Psalm 16:8

Has your faith ever been shaken when you've gone through a difficult and uncertain circumstance? I would be surprised if you said "No," because I think we've all been there. And if we're honest, I believe we'll also admit that we've found ourselves in a place of frustration, wondering what God is doing. We may sometimes even wonder if he's doing anything at all.

When we're in this place, we must shore up our shaky faith, dig down deep to the foundation of our beliefs, and strongly proclaim anew our trust in God. Then we'll be strengthened to face the uncertain circumstances in our lives, rather than being continually shaken by them.

Trusting God:

☐ Requires that we keep our eyes on him and not ourselves or the circumstances around us. *But seek first the kingdom of God and His righteousness, and all these things shall be added to you* (Matthew 6:33).

☐ Invites us to cast our cares on him and to know they are safe in his hands.

Therefore humble yourselves under the mighty hand of God, that He may exalt you in due time, casting all your care upon Him, for He cares for you (1 Peter 5:6-7).

☐ Will bring us his peace, and his peace will calm our fears. *You will keep him in perfect peace, whose mind is stayed on You, because he trusts in You* (Isaiah 26:3).

☐ Takes our shaky faith and strengthens us—and in this strength, we will be steadfast. We will choose to be unshaken. *Therefore, my beloved brethren, be steadfast, immovable, always abounding in the work of the Lord, knowing that your labor is not in vain in the Lord* (1 Corinthians 15:58).

☐ Is letting our faith rest in the One who is unshakeable an unchangeable, and who is the same yesterday, today, and tomorrow. *"For I am the Lord, I do not change; therefore you are not consumed, O sons of Jacob"* (Malachi 3:6).

Jesus Christ is the same yesterday, today, and forever (Hebrews 13:8).

Every good gift and every perfect gift is from above, and comes down from the Father of lights, with whom there is no variation or shadow of turning (James 1:17).

Always Keep the Faith

Sometimes, there are those things that we can never fix …
There are those things that we can never change.
Sometimes, there are those things we'll never understand,
Those things we'll never know the reason why.

Sometimes, there is no answer when we ask, "Why me?"
When we ask, "How could he ever let this be?"

Sometimes,
We face situations beyond our comprehension
That will test our faith and test our trust in him.

There is only one way
To pass the crucial test of faith …
And simply put,
That is to always keep the faith.

Faith is always
Believing what you cannot see
And cannot understand.
Faith is the relationship we are asked
To live out in trust and obedience to the Lord.

Faith is always
Trusting that he's there
And knowing he is
Always in control.

Faith is staying close to him
No matter what comes your way,
And believing he will meet your every need.

Faith is knowing
That he loves you
And will never leave you or forsake you.

Faith believes that in all things
He has a purpose and a plan.

Faith is knowing
You don't have to understand it all
To keep your trust in him.

CHAPTER FIVE

NEVER ALONE

Our hearts beat
In a broken world,
A world that is filled with
Brokenness.
Only God can heal and
Only God can make whole again.

Answers Aren't Everything

You will keep him in perfect peace,
Whose mind is stayed on You,
Because he trusts in You.

—Isaiah 26:3

Too numerous to count are the times I've asked God for answers.

Too numerous to count are the times answers didn't come on my timetable.

The longer I've walked with the Lord, the more I've learned about the process of waiting. Waiting is not a pleasant experience. Waiting tends to be agonizing as it reveals the impatience in our hearts. Waiting is hard.

Yet, waiting can be an invaluable teaching and testing tool—one God often uses in our lives to grow us in our faith. How can something so hard and painful make us grow?

We grow because of what we're doing while we're waiting:

☐ Praying

☐ Seeking wisdom and guidance through Scripture

☐ Watching for direction and movement from God

☐ Learning to trust, practicing our faith, and relying on hope

And we grow because of what God is doing for us while we're waiting: *He gives us peace.* Suddenly, the questioning and the wondering and the waiting become endurable because he answers our faith and trust and hope with *a full indwelling of peace in our hearts.* Peace that strengthens our resolve for the wait. Peace that strengthens us as we continue to seek Him for answers and direction. Peace that assures us that *answers aren't everything, but peace is.*

Across Our Path

> Blessed be the God and Father of our Lord Jesus Christ, the Father of mercies and God of all comfort, who comforts us in all our tribulation, that we may be able to comfort those who are in any trouble, with the comfort with which we ourselves are comforted by God.
>
> —2 Corinthians 1:3-4

We've all had them—"random" meetings with people God brings across our path, seemingly out of the blue. The more we spend time with God, the more we hear his voice. The more we hear his voice, the more we recognize those God-appointed meetings when he wants to use us to help someone. God may nudge us to call someone who is lonely and discouraged. He may want us to walk with someone through a crisis.

A few years ago, my friend Linda met a couple who had recently moved into her neighborhood. The couple had just lost their two-month-old baby boy to Sudden Infant Death Syndrome. The lady, we'll call her Diana, was inconsolable to the point that her husband was seriously considering committing her to a hospital. Linda, having just heard their story, shared it in a prayer request at our women's Bible study. She also shared that Diana and her husband were not Christians and also, didn't have any family in town.

Linda wasn't aware that many years previously, I had given birth to a baby girl who had only lived two days. I knew about loss and grief. I knew the pain of going through that difficult journey. But I also knew the Lord had carried both my husband and me through it. I knew instantly that God had brought Diana across my path, and I told Linda I was supposed to help her. I wanted Diana to know that with time and God's help, we do move from the excruciating place of grief to a place of healing.

Linda called Diana, told her a little of my story, and asked if she would be willing to talk to me. Diana was quite eager to meet.

I met with her many times, and Linda checked on her frequently. Diana was thankful for someone to talk with about her loss and came to know the Lord during that time. When she did, her ability to cope with her loss immediately improved. She now had the hope of seeing her child again. She had hope for herself. She had hope in the Lord. She read her Bible every day, started going to church, and asked us to pray for her husband. He was glad she was doing better, but he wasn't as open to the gospel as Diana had been. We all continued to pray for him.

I met regularly with Diana for over a year, and I'll always remember the day she told me she knew she was doing much better. She was enjoying things again that she hadn't enjoyed for a long time. When we got together for lunch now, she said, we no longer talked just about how she was doing, but also enjoyed small talk about normal things like family, church, and work. When she just wanted to get together as friends, we both knew she had come a long way and was finally in a place of healing.

May we always keep our hearts open to however God wants to use us, and may we always answer his call to walk alongside a hurting person, whether they have lost a job, their health, or a loved one.

Hold Your Peace

And Moses said to the people, "Do not be afraid. Stand still, and see the salvation of the LORD, which He will accomplish for you today. For the Egyptians whom you see today, you shall see again no more forever. The LORD will fight for you, and you shall hold your peace."

—Exodus 14:13-14

The story is familiar and well known: Moses led the Israelite nation out of Egypt, and Pharaoh and his army pursued them. Then God miraculously piled up the waters of the Red Sea and made a way for the Israelites to safely cross over on dry land. The story demonstrates God's power when we are helpless, and reminds us to trust him when we are faced with our back-against-the-wall kind of obstacles.

The Israelites were terrified when they saw the Egyptian army coming toward them as they stood at the sea's edge. Certain destruction seemed to be the only possible outcome, and deliverance appeared to be impossible.

They had already seen God work mightily on their behalf. They had seen his many wonders through the ten terrible plagues in Egypt. They had seen their bondage overturned, and had miraculously been given the freedom to leave Egypt. They should have believed that God was still with them and would save them. Why, then, would they think God had only delivered them from Egypt to have them perish at the hands of the Egyptians? Why would they still believe they were in a situation beyond any possible salvation?

Their cries of despair went up to Moses, who declared, as we read in the verses above, that they should not be afraid. He told them to stand still and watch for God's deliverance. Then he said this: "Hold your peace." They couldn't do one thing for their own deliverance in this impossible situation. But God could, and God did! He spared every life in the Israelite camp and totally destroyed the enemy, bringing the walls of water down upon Pharaoh's army and drowning them.

The Israelites did see the mighty salvation of the Lord! Peace was theirs to have and to hold. It is God's desire for us to have peace when we are afraid, even when it seems the most difficult task in the world. He tells us to stand still and see the salvation of the Lord. He tells us to hold our peace. *Holding God's peace is the deliverance we have from overwhelming worry and fear.*

Prayer Requests

Be anxious for nothing, but in everything by prayer and supplication, with thanksgiving, let your requests be made known to God; and the peace of God, which surpasses all understanding, will guard your hearts and minds through Christ Jesus.

—Philippians 4:6-7

Several years ago, I was in a women's Sunday school class comprised mostly of middle-aged women. I remember a particularly intense season when we had some extremely heavy-duty prayer requests. These ladies came to class knowing we would all listen to each request and pray for every need. One Sunday morning as we went around the room, sharing of prayer requests went like this:

One lady said her divorce was getting uglier, and her son wanted to go live with his father. Her heart was breaking.

The next lady said she suspected her stepdaughter was doing drugs.

One woman shared her mother had just been diagnosed with lung cancer.

Someone asked for prayer for her son, a high-school senior, who had been experiencing a lot of stress as he applied to colleges. He was having severe migraines.

Someone's niece, who was only fourteen, was losing weight. Her parents were worried she was anorexic.

Another shared her son was going to Afghanistan for his second deployment.

Our teacher shared their doctor had called following her husband's routine checkup and asked him to come back to his office to talk about a test result that concerned him. The appointment was coming up later that week.

And then the youngest woman in our class softly said her one-year-old baby had an ear infection.

Our teacher and a few others prayed for each lady's prayer request, and they prayed for each request with the same compassion and intensity, from the mother whose stepdaughter might be doing drugs to the young mother whose baby had an ear infection. God cares about them all. They are all important to him. He heard every request and every prayer in that room. As they shared their requests and then prayed, each lady trusted God to meet her need.

I think all of us mothers can remember the days when we had young children with sore throats and ear infections. The mother whose son was going to Afghanistan again probably wished he was still a little boy, too young to go to war. But our children grow up, and our prayer requests change from ear infections to migraines, to drugs, to eating disorders, and to soldiers going to war. Through it all, we keep taking our cares to God in prayer.

We have the great privilege of sharing our burdens with our brothers and sisters in Christ, and we cherish their prayers for our individual circumstances. We grow lighter from the load we carry because the body of Christ demonstrates its love for one another as we pray for each other. But most of all, we know that our Lord and Savior Jesus Christ cares for each and every prayer request that passes our lips and is uttered in our heart.

What great comfort are the words in Scripture that admonish us to bring our burdens to him and to cast all our cares on the Lord. We can take all things to him in prayer.

> Come to Me, all you who labor and are heavy laden, and I will give you rest.
> —Matthew 11:28

> Casting all your care upon Him, for He cares for you.
> —1 Peter 5:7

FEAR NOT

Fear not, for I am with you; be not dismayed, for I am your God.
—Isaiah 41:10

The greater our trust in God,

The stronger the power we will have over fear.

Have you ever noticed how quickly fear sneaks up on you and sweeps you into a whirlwind of anxious thoughts that quickly spiral out of control? And have you noticed that fear then proceeds to snowball in your mind with a thousand what-ifs that only grow into worse what-ifs?

That is the work of the enemy. He loves that scare tactic and he uses fear often because sadly, it works almost every time.

Sometimes a very small circumstance that is troubling us becomes huge in an instant and fills us with fear. We don't even know how it happened so suddenly. That's the nature of fear. Fear eats away at any peace and stability in our lives. Fear invades every waking moment of our days. Fear takes on a life of its own and undermines our faith and trust in God.

God has not given us a spirit of fear. God gives us courage and strength. That's his nature, and it is what he desires for us. We can walk in boldness through his strength that lives inside of us. Our enemy, Satan, wants us to walk in fear. God, our heavenly Father, who loves us with an everlasting love, desires that we cast out all fear and walk in power and love, and with a sound mind. When we do this, fear is conquered!

When we learn to receive God's strength to fight fear, instead of letting the fear consume us, we can face it as a challenge we know we can overcome.

For God has not given us a spirit of fear, but of power and of love and of a sound mind.
—2 Timothy 1:7

Walking Away and Coming Home Again

For I am persuaded that neither death nor life, nor angels nor principalities nor powers, nor things present nor things to come, nor height nor depth, nor any other created thing, shall be able to separate us from the love of God which is in Christ Jesus our Lord.

—Romans 8:38-39

What causes a person to lose faith and close the door on their relationship with the Lord? What makes some Christians simply walk away?

Disappointment

Divorce

Death of a loved one

Financial loss

Rejection

Sickness

Offense

Most people will likely experience at least one thing on this list, probably more than one. I've heard too many people say that at least one of these experiences was the reason they threw up their hands and walked away.

When a hurt does come along, that's when we really need to be there for each other, to help each other cling to God instead of turning away, to help bring each other back when we lose our way. We need to keep loving, praying, and caring for one another. Satan wants that turning away to happen, and I'm sure he claps his hands in glee when it does.

When something happens to one of God's children that causes us to let go of the grasp we've had on his hand and turn away in anger, hurt, or disbelief, *he never lets us go.* We're still his, no matter what. In spite of the years we may have lived away from him, when we breathe our last earthly breath, we are still his child. We still have the everlasting life he died to give us when we accepted his gift of salvation. We will spend eternity in heaven with the Lord, who never let go of us.

If all of God's children could really grasp this reality and fully understand that he keeps holding onto them even when they let go of him, would it make a difference?

I heard the following testimony in a church service. I was filled with such hope for every person who faces deep pain and moves far away from a close walk with the Lord.

A man in his thirties said he had "stepped out of his relationship with the Lord" after a divorce, and had almost became an alcoholic before someone he worked with invited him to go to church. Feeling at the end of his rope, he decided to go. Then he said these beautiful words: "It was like coming home. I felt the joy I remember knowing when I used to walk closely with the Lord." He admitted he was the one who had walked away. He now realized God had been there all along, waiting for his return.

Have you turned away from him, child of God? He has not turned away from you! He's not the one who moved. He's waiting and longing for you to come back to him.

Tears of Regret

"Be angry and do not sin": do not let the sun go down on
your wrath.

—Ephesians 4:26

Instead of holding on to offenses, we need to let go.

Instead of shaking our fist at God, we need to take His hand.

A few years ago, I visited several grief support groups to observe and gather information to share with the leadership in the counseling ministry at my church. I was amazed at the support and encouragement such groups offered each person who attended.

In one particular session, I met an elderly man who had lost his wife in the last year. He wept bitterly over the loneliness he now experienced. As he tried to wipe away a flow of tears he couldn't stop, he shared that his wife had been the one who'd had friends. Now that she was gone, no one was there for him. He said he had been a bitter, angry man for many, many years, and he admitted that now he felt sorry for holding onto offenses from the past. He had spent most of his adult life angry at God and angry at the people who had hurt him. Now all he had left were tears of regret.

Sometimes, when our response to a deep and painful hurt is anger toward God, that anger keeps us from forgiving God and the one who offended us. It keeps us from letting God heal us. It keeps us from moving forward in our lives. Anger is normal, but staying angry becomes unhealthy and keeps us from healing. Holding on to anger leads to bitterness, depression, and more anger. Ephesians 4 says in verses 26 and 27, *"Be angry, and do not sin": do not let the sun go down on your wrath, nor give place to the devil.*

There are multiple warnings in the book of Proverbs regarding anger and its many dangers. Proverbs 18:19 declares, *A brother offended is harder to win than a strong city, And contentions are like the bars of a castle.*

Our natural, human reaction often leads to an angry shaking of our fists at God for allowing painful events to occur in our lives. But, if we want to find the path to God's healing work in our hearts, we must take his hand and walk with him through the valley of pain. That's how we overcome, work through, and move beyond the pain. That's how we find our healing and experience wholeness again. That's how we demonstrate to our Lord that we are surrendering our lives and our circumstances into his loving care and trusting fully that he will take us past the pain to a new place of hope, peace, and joy.

The enemy wants us to think letting go is simply too hard and painful. But letting go opens the door for God to do his healing work. God's Word strongly teaches that we are to forgive our offender seventy times seven (Matthew 18:21-23). For us, the hard part is arriving at the decision to let it go, but, in letting go, we will reap the sweet fruit of peace and freedom. Yes, we must take a step of faith that requires trusting God, but when we take that step, he gives us the strength to let go. When we obey his Word, he makes it possible for us to do what has seemed too hard … until now.

Those of us sitting around the table offered that elderly man hope, because it is never too late to take that step and let go of the anger, bitterness, and offenses we've been holding in our hearts—even for decades. His countenance changed, and we knew God was softening his heart. The fresh tears he wiped away were now tears of hope.

Renew My Strength

But those who wait on the LORD
Shall renew their strength;
They shall mount up with wings like eagles,
They shall run and not be weary,
They shall walk and not faint.

—Isaiah 40:31

There was a season in my life when several uncertain and difficult circumstances were bearing down on me. I remember feeling the weight of more than I could handle pressing hard on me. I could physically sense a weight pushing down on both my shoulders. My neck grew stiff from the stress. My attempts to change things were futile, and met with disaster—not improvement.

I couldn't understand why nothing seemed to be improving in every scary situation that faced me. I had trouble going to sleep at night because it was hard to relax with so many worries running through my mind. But the more I worried, the worse things seemed.

One night, while tossing and turning in my bed, I remembered the verse in Isaiah 40:31 about God renewing our strength when we trust and wait on him. I asked God to please renew my strength for the next day. I prayed he would help me make it through tomorrow without the weight of the world pressing down on me.

Then I recalled the exact words of the entire verse and found even more comfort. *But those who wait on the LORD shall renew their strength; they shall mount up with wings like eagles, they shall run and not be weary, they shall walk and not faint* (Isaiah 40:31). I repeated this beautiful verse to myself several times and found my strength being renewed as I continued to meditate on the meaning of its words. I fell asleep that night and slept a more peaceful sleep than I had experienced in weeks. God was faithful to renew my strength!

When I woke up the next morning, the weight of the world was no longer pressing down on me. I believed I could run and not be weary, walk and not faint. I felt light enough to fly!

God never intended our burdens to crush us under their weight.
God's promise to those who wait on him is to renew our strength.

Light Inside My Heart

I have come as a light into the world, that whoever believes in
Me should not abide in darkness.

—John 12:46

Sometimes, there is a cloud that hangs over me,
Blocking the light of the joy I am meant to walk in.
The cloud robs me of the strength for each day,
Until I push it away, not letting it stay
And darken a day that's meant to be bright.
I'll push it far away; and if it tries to come back,
I will turn the other way and keep walking in the light.
The Light that came into the world,
Is the Light inside my heart.

Sometimes, we see nothing but dark, hovering clouds. Most of the
time, those clouds are merely attacks of worry, fear, anxiety, and doubt.
Sometimes we're looking at our troubling circumstances through our own
clouded eyes instead of eyes of faith that see what God can do.

Those dark clouds try to rob us of our joy. They try to weaken our faith.
They force us to make a significant choice. Will we choose to stay under the
cloud? Or will we wisely decide to step out in faith and push it away? As
believers and children of God, we must remember to walk toward the light
that's always inside our hearts.

I pray that when these clouds come over us, we will use the strength of
our faith to step out from under their darkness and step into the light of
what God offers us. He is that light, and he wants to shine.

For this to happen, the joy-robbing cloud has to go. I want my light to
shine. Don't you?

Let your light so shine before men, that they may see your good works and glorify your Father in heaven.

—Matthew 5:16

A Path to Healing

He heals the brokenhearted
And binds up their wounds.

—Psalm 147:3

I am so proud of my niece. She suffered the devastating loss of both her parents in a car crash in June 2013. Carla bore the brunt of all that pain. She loved them deeply and had a very special and close relationship with them as their only child.

Carla planned their funeral. She handled their estate and sold their house. She took care of everything. With the passing of time, she has tried to find ways to move on. She looked for a meaningful path to help her heal.

She found purpose in a beautiful yellow lab named Ellie. Ellie is a therapy dog. She has earned her Advance Therapy Dog title through the AKC for one hundred hours of therapy work with the VA. Carla now takes this special dog to visit veterans in the hospital who suffer from Post-Traumatic Stress Disorder.

Ellie loves her work and Carla enjoys it too. She feels like they are giving back in a small way and makes her think of her dad, who had served in the military and cared about veterans. Carla thinks he would be proud that she is doing something to help our nation's vets.

I happen to think they are giving back in a big way, and I am so proud. Carla and Ellie are helping bring vets with PTSD the healing they so desperately need. I admire Carla for her compassion and for the time she gives to help veterans.

Carla walked through a valley of pain and discovered her path to healing by helping others heal. She picked the perfect partner to do this, in her beautiful therapy dog, Ellie.

Jesus narrowed all of God's commandments down to two: *"You shall love the LORD your God with all your heart, with all your soul, and with all your mind"* (Matthew 22:37) and *"You shall love your neighbor as yourself"* (vs. 39). When we've suffered a terrible loss, there is no better way to find our healing than by serving others who are hurting. As we keep his

116

commandment to "love your neighbor as yourself," our hearts go out to others who are suffering, and own pain starts to slowly melt away.

Thank you, Carla and Ellie, for being our example! You do us all proud.

Forgive as We've Been Forgiven

As far as the east is from the west,
So far has He removed our transgressions from us.

—Psalm 103:12

When others have so deeply hurt us,
May we forgive as our Father forgives;
Holding no charge against them,
Tossing offense to the east and the west,
Give mercy as we have been given,
Forgive as we've been forgiven.

I do not write this lightly. I've lived and learned (slowly) that the way we forgive people who have deeply hurt us has no comparison to the forgiveness with which God forgives us.

As I have repeatedly read the story of Joseph's reconciliation (Genesis 37-50) with his brothers, I have been moved each time by the deep compassion and mercy he extended to his brothers. He taught us a valuable and beautiful lesson on forgiveness.

We don't know how long it took Joseph to reach that level of forgiveness after his brothers plotted to murder him, tossed him into a pit, and then sold him into slavery. In my personal opinion, I doubt he came to that forgiving place early on because the hurt was most likely so fresh and deep.

Maybe it was a work God accomplished in his heart through a slow and gradual process over the years he was falsely imprisoned.

Maybe it was when he was released from prison and saw the enormous responsibility and position God had placed him in.

Maybe his heart was opened then to a deeper understanding of God's ways as he learned God's assignment for him was to save the people from famine.

However long it took the healing work of forgiveness to occur in Joseph's heart, I am thankful that he eventually and obediently humbled himself and allowed God to bring this about in him. I have seen many people resist God's work of forgiveness in their lives. The result is always bitterness. Sometimes it is a very evident, outward visible root of bitterness. Sometimes it is a hidden, pushed down, denied form of bitterness. Yet, this bitterness still manages to spill forth in the life of the unforgiving person, usually in the form of anger.

The evidence of genuine forgiveness was displayed when Joseph reunited with his brothers but didn't condemn them for their wrongs. He wept and cried and assured them that what they meant for evil, God meant for good. He took care of them and reestablished relationship with them (Genesis 45).

When others have deeply hurt and betrayed us, may we find it in our hearts to forgive as God taught Joseph to forgive. Following the example of Joseph with his brothers, may we hold no charge against our offenders and betrayers and toss their offenses *as far as the east is from the west* (Psalm 103:12). God wants us to give mercy to others as he has been merciful to us. He wants us to forgive as we have been forgiven.

Lunch with a Friend

Blessed be the God and Father of our Lord Jesus Christ, the Father of mercies and God of all comfort, who comforts us in all our tribulation, that we may be able to comfort those who are in any trouble, with the comfort with which we ourselves are comforted by God.

—2 Corinthians 1:3-4

If you and I met for lunch, I'd probably invite you to meet me at La Madeleine's or Olive Garden, or maybe even at my favorite Mexican restaurant. We'd linger long after we finished our meal and continue talking and catching up on our lives. These long visits with friends can be like a breath of fresh air. Don't you agree?

I lost track of one of my friends for a while. She moved away, and then moved back, but far across town. Eventually, after many delays, we finally managed to meet for lunch at a point halfway between our homes.

After we were seated and were sipping our iced tea, I asked "How are you doing?" Her response of "Fine" didn't sound fine at all. Sure enough, her voice started to tremble and tears welled up in her eyes. Slowly, she began to spell out a difficult situation her family was going through. She also shared that she hadn't told anyone because she was afraid of what others would think.

She admitted, though, that holding it in and not talking to anyone had just made the stress harder to bear. She agreed that when we don't share our burdens we end up *adding burden to burden.*

Here's what I mean by that: when we have difficulty sharing our burdens with others because we don't want to impose our problems on them, we add the burden of carrying the load alone to the original burden created by the situation itself.

God's desire is we come alongside hurting people and help them through the difficult times. What a blessing it is when our friends help us carry life's burdens so we don't have to walk through them alone.

Not Always a Storm

To everything there is a season,
A time for every purpose under heaven:
A time to weep, and a time to laugh;
A time to mourn, and a time to dance.

—Ecclesiastes 3:1,4

Life is not always a storm.

If life was always a storm, the sun would never shine.

I once heard someone say, in reference to the difficult trials we experience in our lives, that all of us are either currently in a storm, at the end of a storm, or getting ready to go into a storm.

I disagree. My life has certainly not been without its storms and trials, but there have been seasons of storms as well as wonderful seasons of calm.

We are not always in a storm or at the fringes of one. Sometimes life is stable and calm. God gives us times when life is just plain good, and we can appreciate all its beauty.

When everything is going along smoothly, we can use those times to find great joy and delight in our close relationship with God. That's when we can take the time to sit at his feet and learn more of him, creating rich "deposits" in our faith account to draw upon in tougher times. Too often, though, we wait to draw close to him only after we get into difficult circumstances. If we fall into a pattern of only calling on the Lord for help when we are in a storm, we may not be prepared to face one when it comes.

The important issue here is consistency in calling upon the Lord every day—whether the skies hold the dark clouds of a storm or they are a brilliant blue with the sun shining brightly. Every day is a day to praise him! Every day is a day to walk hand in hand with the Lord.

When the next storm comes, let him be your refuge, your hiding place, your shelter in the storm. And when the storm is over and life is calm again, be grateful that life is not always a storm. *If life was always a storm, the sun would never shine.*

See Him Now

God is our refuge and strength,
A very present help in trouble.

—Psalm 46:1

Have you ever heard someone say, "Once the storm had passed by and when the trial was over, I could look back and see that God had been with me, after all."? How much more would they have been comforted if they could have seen that God was with them all the way through, from beginning to end. When you find yourself face to face with a difficult trial, as fear descends upon you in those early moments, please know that God wants you to see him now!

Let there be no doubt, God is with us in the midst of our fiery trials. God is always there, never leaving us, never forsaking us (Deuteronomy 31:6). He knows what is happening, and he walks with us through our circumstances from beginning to end, working it out only how he can. Our compassionate Lord wants us to know this at the onset of any trial we experience.

Sometimes we may miss seeing him at the beginning because the storm has taken us by surprise and moved so quickly through our lives, wreaking havoc. When a crisis suddenly and rapidly befalls us, we get swept away in a current of overwhelming fear and anxiety. We forget there is a solid Rock we can cling to, and we find ourselves in the middle of chaos, desperately trying to fix everything ourselves. Our attempts to make everything right are met with failure, and what looms ahead is often more threatening than what has already transpired. When our helplessness and hopelessness leave us with nothing but despair, we cry out to God to rescue us as if he hadn't been there all along.

We go to him as if our crisis caught him unaware, while he wasn't paying attention, and then we worry that the problem is too messy for him to untangle.

How often we forget that he is an all-knowing God, and he precisely and intricately knows all the details of our lives! His desire is for us to see him in the first moment a trial overtakes our lives. He wants us to know, beyond a shadow of doubt, from that first moment on, he is already there working things we cannot see. Our heavenly Father wants us to find comfort and strength in knowing he is our rescuer, our deliverer, and our refuge in life's storms. Psalm 46:1 reminds us, *God is our refuge and strength, a very present help in trouble.*

We will save ourselves a great amount of stress, fear, and anxiety if we cling to the Rock of our salvation every day. Then we will already be holding on to him tightly when the trials crash suddenly and unexpectedly into our lives. Then we will see him and know he is with us, because we have been faithfully walking with and holding the hand of the one who holds us in his hand every day.

God's Word tells us in Isaiah 41:10: *"Fear not, for I am with you; be not dismayed, for I am your God. I will strengthen you, yes, I will help you, I will uphold you with my righteous right hand."* These words assure us that he will be with us in whatever we face in our lives. In the midst of the most fearful times that fall upon us, when we place our faith in his promises ...

We will see him now.

In The Valley

In the valley,
There is only one source of strength,
And it will be found in the nearness
Of the Lord.

In the valley,
His presence will be known
In the midst of every trial,
And all our suffering.

You will not walk alone when your days
Are faced with fear …
The Lord will comfort you
And take you gently by the hand.

In the valley,
You will know the touch of his hand
He'll be tenderly holding you.

CHAPTER SIX

Worship

A heart poured out
Unto the Lord
Is a heart
He delights to fill.

Richly Blessed

When I consider Your heavens, the work of Your fingers,
The moon and the stars, which You have ordained,
What is man that You are mindful of him,
And the son of man that You visit him?
For You have made him a little lower than the angels,
And You have crowned him with glory and honor.
—Psalm 8:3-5

I remember a day the sky was so blue it took my breath away, the sunrise so pink I could only stand in awe. That night, the stars twinkled brighter than ever before, or so it seemed as I gazed enthralled by God's awesome creation.

Surrounded as I am by his constant beauty and all my eyes behold, I proclaim that the greatest wonder of all is the Creator, our Holy, Almighty God. He is the reason I am drawn to drink in a sunrise or sunset. He painted the indescribable, breathtaking blue sky. He placed the stars across the horizon, each one counted, each one named. He made a crown for his creation and called us mankind. He asked us to walk in fellowship with him and enter a relationship described as "after God's own heart."

This is my desire—to pursue the relationship my heavenly Father wants me to have with him. This is my purpose for living, and walking in his purpose brings many blessings. Not the blessings of health, status, wealth, or fame, but the blessings of grace, mercy, love, peace, and joy—only to name a few!

My greatest blessing is I know the God of the universe, who made all things and holds all things in his hands, also holds me in his hands. I am his child, and I delight in knowing there was a moment in time before I was formed in my mother's womb when he thought of me, designed and created me, and ordained my days.

In the days he has given me, I choose to walk with him and build a relationship with the one who gave me life. He gave me physical life in my mother's womb, and he gave me eternal life when I accepted the gift of salvation he provided through his Son, Jesus's death and resurrection. While I am walking day by day with the Lord, I will enjoy each day he has made. I will stand in awe of the beauty he created, and I will count myself richly blessed!

Battles and Praise: Reflections on David

O God, You are my God;
Early will I seek You;
My soul thirsts for You;
My flesh longs for You
In a dry and thirsty land
Where there is no water.

—Psalm 63:1

I read the Psalms more than any other portion of my Bible. I take comfort in and am deeply encouraged by the strong and poetic words written by the major author, a shepherd-warrior king. I keep a long list of favorite verses and passages from the Psalms that I turn to often, and am blessed with each time I read them.

And yet, when I read the story of David's life in the books of I and II Samuel, I see it was wrought with danger, battles, and heartache.

We see David anointed king at a young age by the prophet Samuel, and we see him victoriously kill the giant Goliath with a slingshot. He goes on to become a great warrior. The people's chant *"Saul has slain his thousands, and David his ten-thousands"* puts his life in jeopardy. Their words make David the sworn enemy of King Saul, who becomes jealous and attempts to kill him at every turn. When he is eventually crowned king of Israel, he is engaged in constant war and battles with the enemies that surround God's chosen people, and even with enemies among his own people.

Yes, he writes about battles in the Psalms, but he writes more about victory given by the hand of God. We see God's sovereign hand of guidance and protection, and we hear David declare that our battles belong to the Lord.

Throughout the Psalms, he proclaims that God is *his strength, his refuge, his hiding place, his strong tower, and his shelter in the storm.*

He writes words of praise, worship, and thanksgiving, and in the twenty-third Psalm he beautifully writes …

The Lord is my shepherd I shall not want ...
Surely goodness and mercy shall follow me all the days of my
life ...

We see David rise, fall, and rise again, and we learn from this shepherd-warrior king there is no sin that cannot be washed away and forgiven. We learn that our Holy, Almighty God is a God of healing and restoration.

We see David's battles, and we also see the victories only God can bring. We read this psalmist's praise unto the Lord in words no modern poet has ever been able to duplicate. David teaches us to hide God's Word in our heart, and he teaches us through psalm after psalm that *our hearts are made to worship.*

When I reflect on David, I learn a lot about my God.

Heartbeat

For You formed my inward parts;
You covered me in my mother's womb.
I will praise You, for I am fearfully and wonderfully made;
Marvelous are Your works;
And that my soul knows very well.

—Psalm 139:13-14

One day while I was quietly reading, a distant noise startled me and my heart rate soared. I found myself thinking about my heart, being made keenly aware of its beating, which steadily beats minute after minute, hour after hour, day after day, and year after year.

As I relaxed, and my heart rate slowed to a more normal rhythm, I thought about the wonder of this amazing, beating heart, along with the wonders of all the amazing systems and organs in our body. One word came to my mind: Creator. All of this did not just randomly happen.

I lie in bed listening to the constant rhythm of my beating heart,
And I wonder,
How could anyone not believe in God?
I ponder,
What keeps my heart beating moment to moment,
And all of this miracle of a body that works day after day,
That I am even here?
No, that is not an accident!
I look out the window at earth and sky and wonder,
How could this amazing creation,
How could this intricate design of man
All just be a swirling accident?
The answer is…
It's not!

132

By faith we understand that the worlds were framed by the word of God, so that the things which are seen were not made of things which are visible.

—Hebrews 11:3

Before Our God

Let us therefore come boldly to the throne of grace, that we may obtain mercy and find grace to help in time of need.

—Hebrews 4:16

We can boldly go before our God
And in his presence humbly bow,
Seek his face and call his name …
He is near when we draw near to him.

We were singing "Holy, Holy, Holy" in church recently. I was amazed at how a spirit of worship and oneness filled the room. It seems to happen every time we sing about God's holiness.

When I think about his holiness, I find myself even more amazed that a holy God would let me come to him and call him *Father*. This holy God lets me walk in close relationship with him, and, in fact, greatly desires a closer relationship from me.

All of this is possible because Jesus gave us entrance to his presence through salvation. Jesus's death and resurrection is the only way we can directly connect to the Father. It was Jesus who taught us to pray and to come before our God and call upon him as our heavenly Father.

This relationship builds that position we have with him that is secure and safe. We can take everything to him in prayer with the ease of talking to a father, *our Abba Father.*

Lord,
I am your child,
And this is how I come,
In the presence of all holiness
And the Father of my heart.

Jesus said to him, "I am the way, the truth, and the life. No one comes to the Father except through Me."

—John 14:6

A Heart to Worship

Be still, and know that I am God;
I will be exalted among the nations,
I will be exalted in the earth!

—Psalm 46:10

Worship. Sometimes we make it too complicated, but it doesn't have to be so. God makes it easy.

I have yet to hear a definition of worship that I think is fully adequate. Some things just can't be described in human words. Worship and prayer are two of those indescribable things. Both are intimately personal and both are essential to our walk with the Lord. Both are a privilege we should never take for granted.

Sometimes it's hard for us to worship because of distractions. God makes it easy with a simple invitation to be still and know him and to seek him with all our hearts.

God lovingly and tenderly beckons us and pursues us to draw near, where he is always waiting. Worship is hard to describe, but it's simple, really. *The heart that draws near ... will worship.*

I want the quiet stillness that draws me near to you.
I need the calm serenity that lets me enter in.
With a heart of worship, I come to you,
And accept this invitation to be still and know you.

INADEQUATE WORDS

Enter into His gates with thanksgiving,
And into His courts with praise.
Be thankful to Him, and bless His name.
For the LORD is good;
His mercy is everlasting,
And His truth endures to all generations.

—Psalm 100:4-5

My throat tightens with emotion as I consider how awesome is our God. There are no words to describe him and his wondrous ways. He has blessed me in so many ways, and I find myself continually telling him, "Thank you, thank you, Lord!" Today a river of praise is overflowing from the deep places of my heart.

But "thank you" doesn't begin to express deeply enough or widely enough what I want to say to God for all he's done for me. Thankfully, since my heart is wide open to him, he knows. Some things can be said without words. That's how it is with God.

My words are inadequate, as they often are. I'm glad God knows me and knows what I'm going to say before I say it. He knows the words that are written on my heart but are still left unspoken. He hears them. He hears the silent, wordless prayers that breathe their way to him, because he knows the heart and breath of who I am.

I would be nothing without him, but with him I am all he made me to be. I want to fully live this life he has ordained for me. If today that means awkwardly attempting to express my awe for him, then that is what I will do today, in this moment, with fingers flying across a keyboard and a heart full of worship.

SATISFACTION

The Lord is my Shepherd,
I shall not want.
He makes me to lie down in green pastures;
He leads me beside the still waters.
He restores my soul;
He leads me in the paths of righteousness
For His name's sake.

—Psalm 23:1-3

What satisfies? What brings genuine and fulfilling contentment? For me, it begins with my relationship with the Lord and the benefits that relationship brings:

Knowing I am his

Knowing I am loved

Knowing joy

Knowing peace

Why are we so privileged with such wonderful benefits in our walk with the Lord? Here's my best answer: Just because that's who God is!

☐ He is the lover of our soul.

Yes, I have loved you with an everlasting love; Therefore with lovigkindness I have drawn you.

—Jeremiah 31:3b

☐ He is our joy.

These things I have spoken to you, that My joy may remain in you, and that your joy may be full.
—John 15:11

☐ He is our peace.

Peace I leave with you, My peace I give to you; not as the world gives do I give to you. Let not your heart be troubled, neither let it be afraid.
—John 14:27

LOVE—JOY—PEACE

Do those three words sound familiar? Love, joy, and peace are the first three in the list of the fruit of the Spirit in Galatians 5:22. The more closely we walk with God, the more we will reap love, joy, and peace in great abundance in our lives. They will bring us a wonderful and satisfying contentment we can only know because of him.

Today, let us be grateful! Let us thank him for his goodness to us and for the satisfaction we have in the Lord, who is our shepherd.

Oh, that men would give thanks to the LORD for His goodness,
And for His wonderful works to the children of men!
For He satisfies the longing soul,
And fills the hungry soul with goodness.
—Psalm 107:8-9

Moments of Wonder

Let all the earth fear the LORD;
Let all the inhabitants of the world stand in awe of Him.
For He spoke, and it was done;
He commanded, and it stood fast.

—Psalm 33:8-9

Do you ever have those moments when you slow down, deeply breathe in all that's around you, and are left standing in awe of God, our Creator?

I saw him in the sunrise this morning, as ribbons of violet and pink rose above housetops and golden bursts of sunlight followed closely behind. The brightness soon made me look away, and I thought of the brightness of his glory.

Strolling down my driveway to head out for today's walk, I stopped at the magnolia tree and leaned in close to the rich, creamy, white blossoms and breathed in their sweet aroma. I was amazed at the lavish and stunning flowers all over our tree.

Then, while enjoying my leisurely morning walk, I felt him in the light, warm breeze that drifted soft scents of newly blooming, fragrant honeysuckle all around me. The nearby trickling creek whispered, "He is with you. He is here. He is by your side on this glorious morning walk."

I saw him in the sea of blue skies stretching endlessly above, and, as I drank in this indescribable beauty, I was reminded it was made by the power of his Word.

A field of wildflowers, filled with busy bees furiously at work, called my name. I carefully knelt among them to take in this immeasurable delight and see anew our Creator's handiwork.

The whole earth is blooming in full array around me, and the magnificence and splendor of all God has made takes my breath away.

Don't you love those moments of wonder when you slow down, breathe deeply, and are left standing in awe of God, our Creator?

THE DEEP MYSTERY

When I consider Your heavens, the work of Your fingers,
The moon and the stars, which You have ordained,
What is man that You are mindful of him,
And the son of man that You visit him?
For You have made him a little lower than the angels,
And You have crowned him with glory and honor.

—Psalm 8:3-5

There are times I want to say many things about God and faith, his grace and mercy, and other aspects of this mysterious relationship we have with him, but I can't find the words to adequately express what is stirring in my heart. The more I consider the awesome privilege we have in walking in relationship with him, the more challenging it becomes to explain.

The words are hard to find, because who can explain God? *Why* is he mindful of us? *Why* would he want a close relationship with us?

His Spirit who lives inside of me works in secret ways no one can explain—not the highest scholar, not the greatest theologian. Even the psalmist David grasped for words as he searched, acknowledging that *deep calls unto deep* (Psalm 42:7) as he tried to comprehend what cannot be understood.

By faith, we understand this mystery is the treasure given us by our unseen God. As he lives in us day by day, he continually works in us to build the relationship he designed mankind to have with him—going all the way back to Adam and Eve in the garden of Eden. Throughout the rest of the Bible our story unfolds as we see God still pursuing us, always pursuing us.

Instead of falling for the lies of the enemy and reaching for the forbidden fruit, let us reach for the Lord. Let us reach for God so we can walk in the garden in relationship with him. Let us reach for him *to know him more and to engage this mysterious relationship we have with Him.*

As the deer pants for the water brooks,
So pants my soul for You, O God.
My soul thirsts for God, for the living God.

—Psalm 42:1-2

Deep calls unto deep at the noise of Your waterfalls;
All Your waves and billows have gone over me.
The LORD will command His lovingkindness in the daytime,
And in the night His song shall be with me—
A prayer to the God of my life.

—Psalm 42:7-8

OUR STRENGTH COMES FROM JOY

For the joy of the Lord is your strength.
—Nehemiah 8:10

The story of Nehemiah's rebuilding the walls around Jerusalem after the Israelite kingdoms had been taken into captivity is full of valuable lessons that have taught me a lot about prayer and persistence and believing God will provide.

One of my favorite verses emerges from this story. *For the joy of the Lord is your strength* (Nehemiah 8:10b). I think Nehemiah must have lived this verse, and that's why he accomplished all he did.

While he was in captivity and in the king's court as a cupbearer, the joy of the Lord was his strength.

While he diligently prayed for months and sought God concerning what to do about the broken walls and gates in Jerusalem, the joy of the Lord was his strength.

When he risked his very life and courageously asked King Artaxerxes if he could go to Jerusalem to rebuild the walls, the joy of the Lord was his strength.

When he asked King Artaxerxes for all the supplies and everything he would need to do the job, the joy of the Lord was his strength.

When he surveyed the damage to the walls and devised a plan, the joy of the Lord was his strength.

When Nehemiah and his group of workers were ridiculed for their efforts and threatened with trouble, the joy of the Lord was his strength.

When Nehemiah armed the workers with swords in one hand while they rebuilt the wall with the other, the joy of the Lord was his strength.

When the work was finished and everyone in the city gathered to worship the Lord and give thanks for the rebuilding of the walls, Nehemiah admonished the entire congregation with the words *For the joy of the Lord is your strength* (Nehemiah 8:10).

Is God the source of your joy? Is he the source of your strength? I think we would be wise to declare, as Nehemiah did upon experiencing God's provision and protection, that the joy of the Lord is our strength.

Prayer and Praise

Enter into His gates with thanksgiving,
And into His courts with praise.
Be thankful to Him, and bless His name.
 For the LORD is good;
His mercy is everlasting,
And His truth endures to all generations.

—Psalm 100:4-5

It was one of those days when the needs on my prayer list were so intense and urgent that I cried many tears as I laid those petitions at God's feet, calling upon him to move in a mighty way.

We all have those seasons when prayer is a true battle. We don't know how God will answer. We know he is working. We know he wants us to pray. But there is more to praying than praying.

On that particular day, I forgot there is more to prayer than simply saying the words. After I prayed, I became busy with one thing after another. Later in the day, I was preoccupied as I drove down the road with to-do lists running through my head. Out of nowhere, I realized in the midst of my earlier prayer battle, I had forgotten something very important.

I forgot to worship God! I forgot to praise him!

I had begged him to work in this situation and in that circumstance and on that person's behalf, but I forgot to give him my praise.

When I returned home and was alone I said, "Father, I forgot to praise you then, but I praise you now."

He knows, of course, that praise for him is always abiding in my heart—it's how I try to live my life. I want praise to be a habit. It's important, when I go to him in prayer, that I acknowledge the great and wonderful God he is and bless him from the depths of my heart.

That day, I was swept away by all the battles that needed to be fought in prayer, none of which I could win, but all of which were in his hands. And all were reasons to give him all my praise.

Let's not forget to praise him every day!

Our Father in heaven, hallowed is your name!

Holy, Holy, Holy, Lord God Almighty!

EARLY

My voice You shall hear in the morning, O LORD;
In the morning I will direct it to You,
And I will look up.

—Psalm 5:3

When did you first meet the Lord today? When did you make that vital choice to pause and be still and connect your heart to his?

Connection *is a wonderful way to start every new day.*

Did you thank him for this day? Did you thank him that you belong to him? Did you thank him for loving you unconditionally?

Gratitude *is a wonderful way to start every new day.*

Did you invite him to go with you through this day? Did you ask for his wisdom and guidance for all that lies ahead in the uncertainty of the day?

Being humble *is a wonderful way to start every new day.*

Did you acknowledge him as Lord of your life in every aspect of your life? Did you praise him for who he is?

Praise *is a wonderful way to start every new day.*

When we miss this important connection early in the day, the places of our heart that are meant to be filled with the Lord can too easily become like a desert, dry and thirsty. But when we longingly thirst for him, he will fill us up with himself, and we can face each new day walking in the joy and strength of our Lord.

Delight in the Ways of the Lord

And his heart took delight in the ways of the Lord.

—2 Chronicles 17:6

There is a very special story in 2 Chronicles, an Old Testament book that further details what we've already learned in 2 Kings as we follow the lineage of David. As we watch the Israelite people move farther away from God with a parade of bad kings, we also see a few good kings rise among the heap.

Jehoshaphat was one of the few good kings, and in 2 Chronicles 17 there is a portion about him that speaks to my heart:

> Now the Lord was with Jehoshaphat, because he walked in the former ways of his father David; he did not seek the Baals, but sought the God of his father, and walked in His commandments and not according to the acts of Israel. Therefore the Lord established the kingdom in his hand; and all Judah gave presents to Jehoshaphat, and he had riches and honor in abundance. And his heart took delight in the ways of the Lord; moreover he removed the high places and wooden images from Judah.

—2 Chronicles 17:3-6

His heart took delight! This king's heart took delight in the ways of the Lord!

One day, as I read these verses, I was sitting by the window, preparing my heart for prayer, and God delighted me with the swirling of leaves outside, blown and tossed about on the autumn breeze. I watched leaf after leaf ride the wind, traveling airborne across the yard.

Sunlight scattered like gold on the oak tree in the corner of the back yard.

My gaze focused on the beauty of trees and sky, a rabbit hopping into the garden, and the doves that were already eating the birdseed I'd just

148

tossed on the ground. I chose to memorize this scene and store it away for the coming winter months.

My thoughts then returned to the verses I'd read earlier, and I knew I wanted those same words to be said of me—that my heart takes delight in the ways of the Lord, ways that are higher than ours, because he is an awesome God.

I closed my eyes to pray. *I'm not a king, but I will follow the example of King Jehoshaphat. I will delight in the ways of the Lord. I will start with delighting in all the beauty that he provided before my eyes as I watched the golden sunlight dance across the yard.*

Won't you, too, follow the example of the good king Jehoshaphat, whose heart took delight in the ways of the Lord?

When I Breathe

Draw near to God and He will draw near to you.

—James 4:8

When do you experience God's nearness?

This question was asked in a Bible study group discussion as we talked about the subject of walking in a close relationship with God.

Everyone who had gathered around the long rectangle table with Bibles and workbooks had something to say about it, but their answers varied.

- *When I see a sunset, I feel his presence.*

- *Definitely a stroll on the beach.*

- *When I walk in the nearby woods.*

- *In my quiet time each day.*

- *When there is no one else in the house and it is just God and me.*

- *Over coffee each morning.*

The answer burning in my heart was *When I breathe. Oh, yes, and with every breath and beat of my heart and every step I take—his nearness is constant to me!*

What I know with all certainty is if we seek him, we will find him because he is already there. *He is near*—it is his place in your life.

Our life should be in the position of perpetually drawing near. Our walk with the Lord is about relationship, a relationship that is as close as *when you breathe.*

Take a deep breath.

Inhale. Then exhale slowly and breathe these words, "Lord, I know you are near."

And you will seek Me and find Me, when you search for Me with all your heart.

—Jeremiah 29:13

So that they should seek the Lord, in the hope that they might grope for Him and find Him, though He is not far from each one of us; for in Him we live and move and have our being, as also some of your own poets have said, "For we are also His offspring."

—Acts 17:27-28

HAND IN HAND

Today I walked with my Father,
Hand in hand along the way.
We talked and shared precious moments,
Down a long and winding road.

"Do you see how brilliant and beautiful
Your sun shines in the sky?
And those flowers by the roadside,
Do they always bloom so bright?
Look, do you see that eagle,
Do you see how high it soars?"

Hand in hand we spent the day, hand in hand along the way.
I pointed out the beauty in all that he had made,
While many times I was overwhelmed,
I'm with him!
He's with me!
We stopped, he said to rest a while,
And I followed his upward gaze.
He took my hand and told me
To watch that eagle in the sky.

He looked deep into my eyes,
And straight into my heart.
I could not breathe or move
As his Spirit surrounded me.
He spoke words of life to me—
Words I will never forget:
"I have given you wings like an eagle,
Now it is time for you to fly!"

As I began to understand the meaning of his words,
His hand slipped out of mine and he turned to walk away.
I did not move, my hand yet warm,
His presence still with me.

He called to me as he walked away,
"I will be your strength,
I am with you always,
I will never let you go!"

How could I not believe
With eagle's wings I'll fly?
His Spirit strong within me,
Oh, yes, you'll see me flying high!

ABOUT THE AUTHOR

Kathy Cheek has more than ten years' experience as a freelancer writing for the Christian market including LifeWay, Walk Thru the Bible, David C Cook, and Group Publishing, as well as online at Thoughts About God, Christian Devotions, and In Courage.

Kathy lives what she writes, and she writes from the heart. She loves Jesus who saved her and draws her near every day, and she wants you to know more deeply this foundational love and relationship. Kathy writes Bible-based, faith-filled devotions that will encourage you to develop a strong and lasting trust in the Lord. You can read more of her devotions at her website Devotions from the Heart at www.kathycheek.com.

When she isn't writing, Kathy thrives on quiet walks on the trail along the creek and woods near her home. She and her husband enjoy long country drives where they love exploring small Texas towns.

She and her husband of thirty-four years live in a suburb of Dallas, Texas. They have two daughters, one son-in-law, and a grandson who also reside in the Dallas area.

54352586R00095

Made in the USA
Columbia, SC
29 March 2019